Student Cookbook

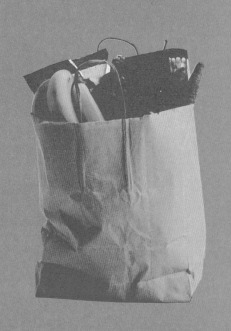
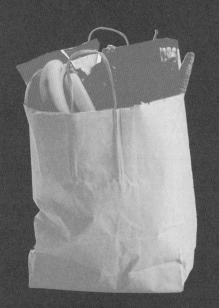

Student Cookbook

OVER 100 EASY AND ECONOMICAL DISHES FOR HUNGRY STUDENTS

This edition published in 2011
LOVE FOOD is an imprint of Parragon Books Ltd

Parragon
Queen Street House
4 Queen Street
Bath BA1 1HE, UK

ISBN: 978-1-4454-3370-7

Printed in China

Internal design by Andrew Easton @ Ummagumma
Introduction by Dominic Utton

With thanks to our student taste team: Laura Dickson, Lindsey Frost, Johanna Granville-Edmunds, Charlotte Hawken, Sophie Parker, Chemaine Shehadeh, Dan Toy, Anthony Trigo and Fiona Wong

Notes for the Reader
This book uses both metric and imperial measurements. Follow the same units of measurement throughout; do not mix metric and imperial. All spoon measurements are level: teaspoons are assumed to be 5 ml, and tablespoons are assumed to be 15 ml. Unless otherwise stated, milk is assumed to be full fat, eggs and individual vegetables are medium, and pepper is freshly ground black pepper.

The times given are an approximate guide only. Preparation times differ according to the techniques used by different people and the cooking times may also vary from those given. Optional ingredients, variations or serving suggestions have not been included in the calculations.

Recipes using raw or very lightly cooked eggs should be avoided by infants, the elderly, pregnant women, convalescents and anyone suffering from an illness. Pregnant and breastfeeding women are advised to avoid eating peanuts and peanut products. Sufferers from nut allergies should be aware that some of the ready-made ingredients used in the recipes in this book may contain nuts. Always check the packaging before use. Vegetarians should be aware that some brands of the ready-made ingredients used in the recipes in this book may contain animal products. Always check the packaging before use.

Picture acknowledgements
The publisher would like to thank Getty Images for permission to reproduce copyright material:
cover (front and spine) and pages 2, 5, 6, 8, 9, 11, 12, 14, 44, 76, 104, 136 and 164

contents

introduction

So, you've finally done it. You've left home, struck out on your own. Congratulations: you've become a student. The hallowed halls and dreaming spires of academia are calling, a wide world of learning beckons.

Well, something like that, anyway.

Going to university is not just about libraries, labs and lectures – let's be honest, if it was, then the whole thing wouldn't be half as much fun. No: the real point of student life is what happens when you're away from your books. These years are about leaving the comforts (and restrictions) of home and experiencing stuff for yourself. There will be societies to join, teams to get involved in. There's a (very) good chance the Union bar will become a place you're intimately familiar with. There will be an indecent number of parties, an embarrassing number of nights out. Over the next three or four years, you're going to have a better, more active, more exciting social diary than you will ever experience again.

In short, you're going to have the time of your life.

Forget what they say about students having nothing better to do than laze around watching afternoon telly and gazing at their navels: once you're at university you'll soon find that there's simply not enough hours in the day to cram it all in (even if that does include a bit of afternoon telly). You're independent now – nobody's going to tell you what time to go to bed or what time to get up (though your lecturers might have some 'suggestions' about this), nobody's going to dictate where and how often you go out... and nobody's going to tell you what to eat.

You do have some responsibilities, of course. Living on a budget is never easy, coping with doing your own washing can take a bit of practice, and, given why you're there in the first place, some work may even have to be done. And, of course, amidst the general madness of student life, you're going to have to eat. Not only eat – you're going to have to cook. Once you reach uni, Mum's three square meals a day become a distant, impossible memory, and unless you learn your way around a kitchen, the sad result can be the kind of diet that would embarrass a dog.

It's tricky, we know. When you've got so much to do, taking the time out to prepare gourmet-quality meals can seem a pretty low priority. And when the pittance you're supposed to live on barely covers keeping you in haircuts and decent trainers, blowing your hard-earned student loan on anything more nutritious than a takeaway burger can seem like pure wanton extravagance. But it needn't be so. There can be so much more to student cooking than ketchup pasta and cheesy peas. A balanced diet does not mean equal parts bread and jam. Putting together fresh, wholesome meals can be fast, easy and, most importantly, cheap. And, crucially, it can involve a minimum of washing up afterwards too.

Learning to cook for yourself is not only healthier than a diet of takeaways and ready meals, it's easier on the overdraft too. For the price of a couple of microwave curries and a late-night kebab you can eat fresh food for a week. Getting stuck into the kitchen can be a great way to unwind at the end of the day, it can be a fantastic means of socializing with your fellow house- or hall-mates and it's a pretty sure way to impress any potential dates. And, of course, knowing you're eating properly will give your parents one less thing to worry/nag about.

It really is easier than you think. Don't be intimidated. Yeah, so there's always going to be someone in your halls who claims he can whip up a Béarnaise sauce quicker than you can pour a beer – like, whatever. As the recipes inside this book show, a repertoire of simple, wholesome, well-prepared meals is always going to be every bit as impressive as that fabulously complicated (and probably fictional) solitary cordon bleu creation he'll manage once a term. With a little practice, you'll soon be making food that looks and smells so good you won't know whether to eat it or kiss it.

One last thing before you get busy with the pots and pans: remember that being able to put together a meal is just a part of student cooking. After all, being a student – whether you're living in halls or sharing a house – is about learning to live together. By all means show what you can do in the kitchen, but remember that it is a shared space. The last thing you want is fights over fridge space and oven rights. Everyone's heard the stories of stolen eggs, watered-down orange juice, people spiking each other's bread with salt... and of course there's the now infamous note left on one shared student fridge: 'Keep out,' it read, 'I lick my cheese.' You really don't want to have to be reading that first thing in the morning!

The student kitchen can be so much more than a place to boil the kettle or scrounge some toast: it can be the centre of your home life. Cooking for your house- or hall-mates will forge strong bonds – and should ensure you get a few free meals back too. And most of all, it's fun! So grab an apron, open up and tuck in. Trust us: there's really nothing like a bit of home cooking for finally shaking that 14-hour hangover...

shopping

If you want to whip up a storm in the kitchen, you're going to have to hit the shops first. Find what works for you – you may prefer to shop for a few bits each day, do a weekly grocery shop or save up for a monthly supermarket sweep. Alternatively, you could avoid the supermarket altogether and shop at your local market. Whatever you decide to do, the following tips should help you to make the most of your finances.

1. Set a budget – work out how much you can afford to spend on food (remembering to factor in the odd canteen meal or takeaway) and stick to it. You may want to have a separate budget for alcohol!

2. Plan your meals – making a menu plan for the week ahead and only buying what you actually need (rather than what you think you need) is one of the easiest ways to cut your food bill. It doesn't have to be too restrictive either – you can juggle the meals around during the week depending on what you feel like eating.

3. Write a list – there's nothing worse than getting home and realizing that you've forgotten to buy a vital ingredient. Having a list will also stop you from making those impulse purchases that bump up your shopping bill. Take a pen and tick off the items as you put them in your basket or trolley.

4. Check your larder – before you go shopping, have a quick rummage through your cupboards. You never know what hidden gems you might find in there, plus there's no point in buying something that you already have. Look in the fridge and throw away anything that's gone off to make room for your new purchases.

5. Don't shop for food on an empty stomach – this is a definite no-no for anyone on a budget because you'll be much more likely to give in to temptation and buy things that aren't on your list if you're hungry.

6. Give yourself enough time to shop – if you're in a rush, you're much more likely to end up panic buying and reaching for the first thing you see, rather than considering which items are the best value. Take a few moments to compare similar products and always check the 'best before' and 'use by' dates on perishable items.

7. Don't buy everything at once – don't rush out and buy every item on the storecupboard staples list (see page 10) straightaway. Start with a few basics and build up your stocks as you try new recipes. There's no point buying a load of spices if you never cook anything more adventurous than pasta and sauce! Similarly, if an ingredient is new to you, buy a small pack to see if you like it before you stock up.

8. Don't be put off trying supermarket 'basic' ranges – just because your Mum buys the premium version of a product, doesn't mean that you should! Branded foods might seem familiar and cosy, but the reality is that the economy equivalent is more suited to the student wallet. Besides, we reckon you won't be able to taste the difference anyway.

9. Don't buy more than you need – super-size packs aren't such a good deal if you end up chucking half of their contents away because they've gone off before you have the chance to finish them! If you are buying in bulk, consider clubbing together with a few mates so you can split the cost, or stick to non-perishable items that you know you will use.

10. Grab a bargain – it can pay to shop at the end of the day when items are being marked down for a quick sale (although in these days of 24-hour shopping this is less commonplace than it used to be). Many stores have a section where they keep reduced items, particularly fresh foods that are close to their 'best before' or 'use by' dates. Also, look out for discount baskets containing end-of-line products at a special price.

11. Be a coupon queen or king – when you're flicking through magazines or newspapers, keep an eye out for money-off coupons. Cut out any for products that you usually buy and stash in your wallet until your next shop.

12. Make friends with your freezer – it's not just there for oven chips and fish fingers! Frozen vegetables are just as nutritious as fresh ones and fresh sliced bread can be frozen and taken out a slice at a time as you need it. You can also freeze any leftover soups and casseroles to eat another day.

13. Buy loose fruit and vegetables – they tend to be cheaper than pre-packed ones. Also, as you only have to buy as many as you actually need, you're less likely to discover mouldering vegetables in your cupboard a few weeks along the line.

14. Consider internet shopping – most supermarkets offer an on-line order and delivery service for groceries. It's especially useful if you don't have a car as you can order bulky or heavy items that you wouldn't be able to lug home yourself. There's usually a small delivery fee but you could always do a joint shop with some of your fellow students and share the cost.

15. Don't get stuck in a rut – it's easy to get into the habit of eating the same foods week in, week out. Banish boredom by varying your meals – the recipes in this book should certainly provide plenty of inspiration!

storecupboard staples

The list below gives a number of basic pantry items that are useful to get you started. As you work through the recipes in this book, you'll quickly build up a stash of ingredients and, after a while, you'll find that you already have many of the items you need to try a new recipe.

Cans and jars

Tomatoes
Beans, such as baked beans, kidney
 beans and butter beans
Fish, such as tuna, salmon and
 anchovies
Coconut milk
Olives
Honey
Peanut butter

Bottles

Vegetable or groundnut oil
Olive oil

Condiments

Salt
Pepper

Dried herbs, such as oregano,
 thyme and bay leaves
Dried spices, such as ground
 coriander, cumin, paprika and
 cinnamon
Dried chilli flakes
Curry powder/paste
Tomato ketchup
Soy sauce
Worcestershire sauce
Mustard
Vinegar

Dry goods

Flour   Pasta   Cereal
Oats   Rice
Sugar   Noodles
Stock cubes/bouillon powder

Fresh

Milk
Butter/margarine
Cheese
Eggs

Frozen

Fruit and vegetables, such
 as frozen berries, peas and
 sweetcorn
Bread

Other supplies

Kitchen paper
Clingfilm/polythene bags
Aluminium foil
Bin liners
Cleaning products

clean & tidy

Okay, so your average student kitchen is unlikely to be a haven of hygiene but it doesn't have to be a grotto of grime either! Cleaning doesn't have to be a chore if you keep on top of it. The tips below should point you in the right direction and help you to avoid a nasty bout of food poisoning.

- Wipe down the surfaces before and after cooking using a clean sponge or cloth.
- Sweep the flour regularly – unless you want to share your kitchen with rodents!
- Wipe up any spills on the hob after use. It's much easier to clean them off straightaway than to leave them until they're practically welded on.
- Avoid arguments by organizing a cleaning rota so that one person doesn't end up rushing around cleaning up after everybody.
- Wash your hands regularly before and during cooking, especially if you've been handing raw meat and poultry. Dry them on a clean towel – not one you found in a heap on the floor!
- Check your fridge temperature – it should be below 5°C/41°F in order to keep your food nicely chilled.
- Clear out the fridge regularly and throw away anything that's past its best. You don't want to be pouring sour, lumpy milk onto your breakfast cereal!
- Keep cooked and raw foods separate in the fridge. Ideally, raw meat, poultry and fish should be stored on the bottom shelf so it can't drip onto any food underneath.
- Leftovers should be cooled first, then stored in the fridge in airtight containers.
- Do not re-freeze foods that have already been frozen and defrosted.

kitchen safety

Kitchens can be really dangerous places, and the student kitchen is no exception. With hazards including sharp knives, boiling water, electrical appliances and hot surfaces, not to mention the fact that it's populated by a rowdy group of novice cooks, it's probably the deadliest room in the entire house! But don't be alarmed – by following the tips below you can minimize the risks to yourself and others.

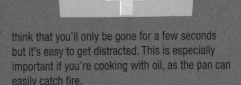

- Mop up any spills before someone slips on them.

- Always use (dry) oven gloves to handle hot pans or dishes.

- Carry knives by your side with the tip pointing downwards.

- Don't leave sharp items, such as knives, in a sink full of water. The next person to put their hand in there might get a nasty surprise!

- If you're using the hob, make sure that your pan handle is positioned to the side, rather than the front, so that it can't easily be knocked off.

- Don't place flammable items, such as tea towels, close to the hob.

- Grill pans full of accumulated fat are a potential fire hazard, as well as being disgusting! By lining the pan with aluminium foil and removing and discarding after each use, you'll never have to face the chore of cleaning a grotty grill pan again. Do not line the grill rack as this will stop the fat from draining off and may cause flare ups.

- Don't wander off while you're cooking, leaving a hot pan on the hob or anything under the grill. You might think that you'll only be gone for a few seconds but it's easy to get distracted. This is especially important if you're cooking with oil, as the pan can easily catch fire.

- If a pan does catch fire, do not attempt to move it but do turn off the heat if it's safe to do so (i.e. if you don't have to lean over the pan to reach the controls). Cover with a fire blanket or damp tea towel and leave until cool. Never throw water over a pan fire or use a fire extinguisher.

- If an electrical appliance is on fire, pull out the plug if it's safe to do so, or switch off at the fusebox. If this doesn't stop the fire, try to smother it with a fire blanket or use a carbon dioxide extinguisher.

- If you can't deal with a fire yourself, leave the kitchen, closing the door behind you, and call 999. Make sure that others are aware of the fire (break the glass on the fire alarm if there is one) and evacuate the building.

about this book

Further hints and tips give useful advice and offer guidance to the beginner cook.

Number of servings. Most recipes can easily be halved or doubled, depending on how many people you've got to feed.

These symbols give at-a-glance information about the recipe, such as whether it is suitable for vegetarians. For further information, see the key below.

Each recipe includes a full list of ingredients, with preparation instructions where necessary. Assemble all your ingredients before you start cooking.

KEY

Healthy

Veggie

Speedy

Cheap

Impressive

One pot

Spicy

Some of the recipes have been tested by our specially selected student taste team. You'll find their comments (and marks out of ten!) here.

All the recipes feature step-by-step instructions, making them easy to follow – even for novice cooks! Always read through the recipe before you start, noting the timings and the equipment needed.

All the recipes are accompanied by a colour photograph of the finished dish

pasta salad

Serves 2

Ingredients
100 g/3½ oz dried pasta shapes
1 tbsp olive oil, plus extra if needed
1 tbsp mayonnaise
1 tbsp natural yogurt
2 tbsp pesto
200 g/7 oz canned tuna, drained and flaked
200 g/7 oz canned sweetcorn kernels, drained
2 tomatoes, peeled, deseeded and chopped
½ green pepper, deseeded and chopped
½ avocado, stoned, peeled and chopped
salt and pepper

Pasta salads are incredibly versatile – just add any salad ingredients you have to hand. Vegetarians could use drained canned beans in place of the tuna.

Method
1 Cook the pasta in a large saucepan of boiling water for 8–10 minutes, until just tender. Drain, return to the saucepan and add the oil. Toss well to coat, then cover and leave to cool.
2 To make the dressing, whisk the mayonnaise, yogurt and pesto together in a jug, adding a little oil if needed to achieve the desired consistency. Add a pinch of salt and season to taste with pepper.
3 Mix the cooled pasta with the tuna, sweetcorn, tomatoes, green pepper and avocado, add the dressing and toss well to coat. Transfer to an airtight container for a packed lunch.

STUDENT TASTE TEAM
Name: Dan Toy
Studying: Writing for Publication, Performance and Media
At: Pratt Institute, USA
Marks: 9/10
Comments about dish: this recipe necessitated inexpensive ingredients and was easy to make

62

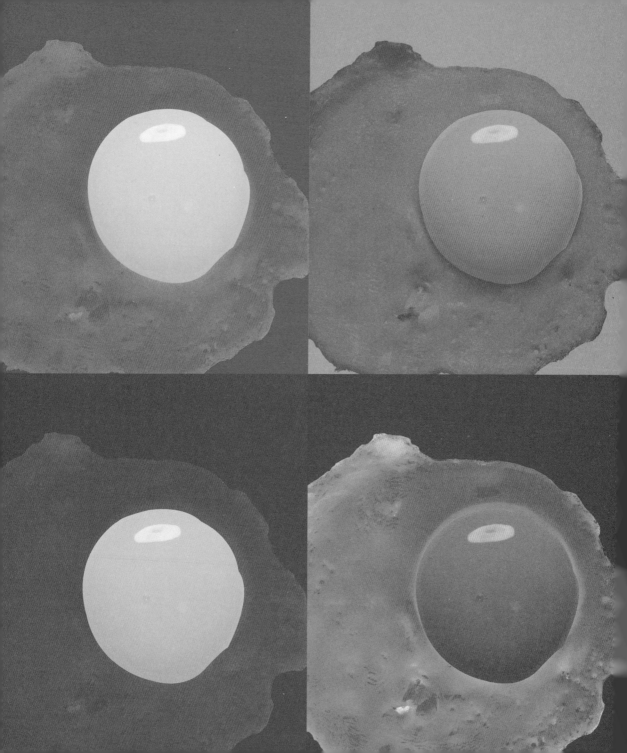

the big breakfast

It's tempting to skip breakfast in favour of extra snoozing time, but eating a hearty brekkie really is the best start to the day. It's the perfect opportunity to fuel up ready for a hectic day's studying, especially if you're not sure if you'll get a chance to stop for lunch. Whether you're after a recipe for a quick weekday breakfast or a lazy Sunday brunch, this chapter contains all sorts of tempting treats to entice you out from under the duvet.

fruity yogurt with granola

Serves 1

Ingredients
200 g/7 oz rolled oats
2 tbsp clear honey
2 tbsp pumpkin seeds
2 tbsp sunflower seeds
2 tbsp chopped walnuts
1 small ripe pear, peeled,
   cored and chopped
½ ripe mango, peeled, stoned and chopped
125 g/4½ oz natural yogurt

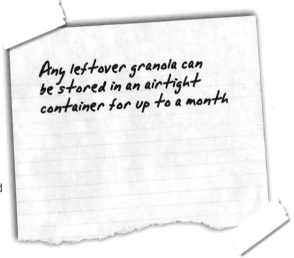

Any leftover granola can be stored in an airtight container for up to a month

Method
1 Preheat the oven to 180°C/350°F/Gas Mark 4.
2 For the granola, mix the oats and honey together in a bowl and spread out on a baking sheet. Bake in the preheated oven for 10–15 minutes, stirring a couple of times, until the oats are lightly browned, then remove from the oven and leave to cool.
3 Place the seeds in a mortar and briefly grind with a pestle to break them into smaller pieces. Mix with the cooled oats and the walnuts.
4 To assemble, put half the pear and mango in a glass and top with half the yogurt and a spoonful of granola. Repeat with the remaining fruit and yogurt and top with more granola.

fruity porridge

Serves 4

Ingredients

175 g/6 oz jumbo porridge oats

55 g/2 oz oatmeal

pinch of salt (optional)

850 ml/1½ pints milk

55 g/2 oz dried apricots, chopped

25 g/1 oz sunflower seeds

2 bananas, peeled and sliced

Try adding a handful of frozen berries a couple of minutes before the end of the cooking time. Frozen berries are much cheaper than fresh ones, but just as tasty!

Method

1 Place the oats and oatmeal in a saucepan together with the salt, if using, and stir in the milk. Place over a gentle heat and cook, stirring, for 7–8 minutes, or until the oats thicken.

2 Spoon the porridge into individual dishes and scatter over the dried apricots and sunflower seeds. Top with the banana slices and serve.

STUDENT TASTE TEAM

Name: Fiona Wong

Studying: IB Diploma

At: Renaissance College, Hong Kong

Comments about dish: Fast and convenient – a wonderful choice if you are on a diet

Marks: 7/10

citrus zinger

Serves 1

Ingredients

1 pink grapefruit

1 orange

½ lemon

½ lime

lime slice, to decorate

Method

1 Cut the grapefruit and orange in half using a sharp knife.

2 Using a lemon squeezer, juice the grapefruit, orange, lemon and lime and pour into a glass. Stir, decorate with a lime slice and serve immediately.

banana breakfast shake

Serves 2

Ingredients

2 ripe bananas, chopped

200 ml/7 fl oz low-fat natural yogurt

125 ml/4 fl oz milk

½ tsp vanilla essence

honey, for drizzling

Method

1 Put the bananas, yogurt, milk and vanilla essence into a tall beaker.

2 Using a hand-held stick blender, process until smooth.

3 Pour into glasses, drizzle with honey and serve immediately.

blueberry bliss

Serves 2

Ingredients

250 g/9 oz fresh or frozen blueberries

500 g/1 lb 2 oz vanilla-flavoured yogurt

½ large banana, chopped

lemon juice or honey, to taste

Method

1 Put the blueberries, yogurt and banana into a tall beaker.

2 Using a hand-held stick blender, process until smooth.

3 Taste and add a little lemon juice or honey, if wished, then process again. Pour into glasses and serve immediately.

mango smoothie

Serves 1

Ingredients

1 ripe mango, peeled, stoned and sliced

1 tsp clear honey

200 ml/7 fl oz freshly squeezed orange juice

2 tbsp natural yogurt

Method

1 Put the mango, honey, orange juice and yogurt into a tall beaker.

2 Using a hand-held stick blender, process until smooth.

3 Pour into a glass and serve immediately.

melon & strawberry crunch

Serves 4

Ingredients

25 g/1 oz rolled oats

25 g/1 oz oat bran

2 tbsp toasted flaked almonds

25 g/1 oz ready-to-eat dried apricots, finely chopped

½ melon, such as Galia

225 g/8 oz strawberries, hulled

150 ml/5 fl oz milk or orange juice, to serve (optional)

Method

1 Put the rolled oats and oat bran in a bowl and stir in the almonds and dried apricots.

2 Discard the skin and seeds from the melon and cut into small bite-sized pieces. Halve the strawberries if large.

3 Divide the rolled oat mixture between 4 individual bowls, then top with the melon and strawberries. If liked, serve with either milk or orange juice.

grilled cinnamon oranges

Serves 4

Ingredients

4 large oranges

1 tsp ground cinnamon

1 tbsp demerara sugar

Method

1 Preheat the grill to high. Cut the oranges in half and discard any pips. Using a sharp knife or a curved grapefruit knife, carefully cut the flesh away from the skin by cutting around the edge of the fruit. Cut across the segments to loosen the flesh into bite-sized pieces that will then spoon out easily.

2 Arrange the orange halves, cut-side up, in a shallow ovenproof dish. Mix the cinnamon with the sugar in a small bowl and sprinkle evenly over the orange halves.

3 Cook under the preheated grill for 3–5 minutes, or until the sugar has caramelized and is golden and bubbling. Serve immediately.

Most fruits are available year-round but bear in mind that they will be cheaper when they're in season.

croissant pudding with peaches

Serves 4

Ingredients
6–8 stale croissants
300 g/10½ oz canned peaches
500 ml/18 fl oz milk
3 eggs
6 tbsp granulated sugar
icing sugar, for dusting

This dish is perfect for a lazy weekend brunch. Try using different canned fruits in place of the peaches.

Method

1 Preheat the oven to 190°C/375°/Gas Mark 5.

2 Halve the croissants and put them into a baking dish in layers. Drain the peaches, reserving the juice, then cut into pieces and spread out over the croissants.

3 Put the milk, eggs and 4 tablespoons of the granulated sugar into a jug and beat with a fork.

4 Pour the milk and egg mix slowly and evenly over the croissants, so that they soak up the liquid. Leave to stand for about 5 minutes, pressing the croissants into the milk every so often.

5 Sprinkle with the remaining granulated sugar, which will caramelize lightly when baking.

6 Bake in the preheated oven for 25 minutes. The pudding is ready when it has risen by about a third. Dust the top with icing sugar. Spoon onto plates and pour over some of the peach juice from the can.

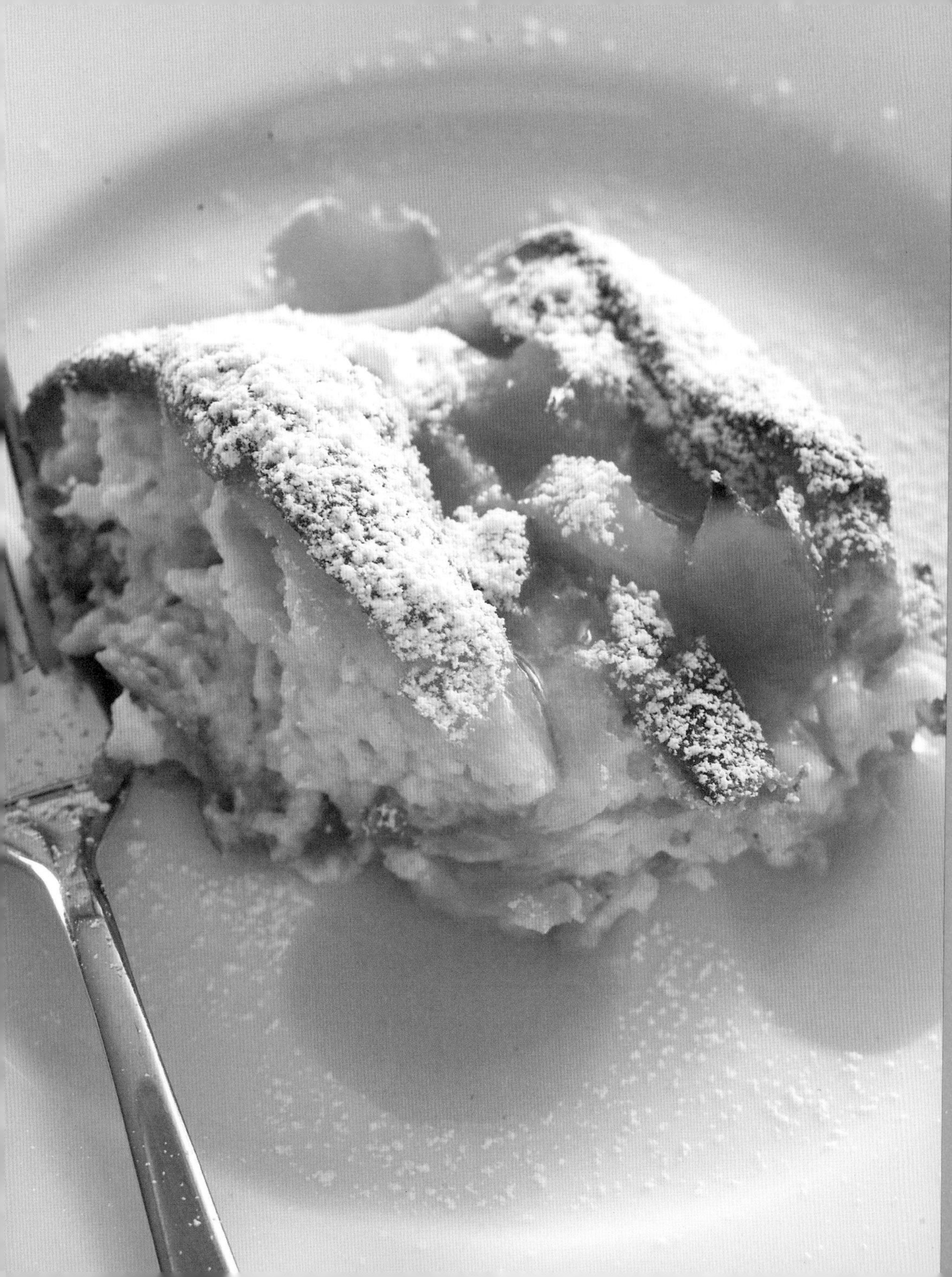

sweet scrambled eggs with cornflakes

Serves 1

Ingredients

2 large eggs

2 tbsp granulated sugar,
  plus extra for sprinkling

50 g/1¾ oz cornflakes

1 tbsp butter

pinch of cinnamon

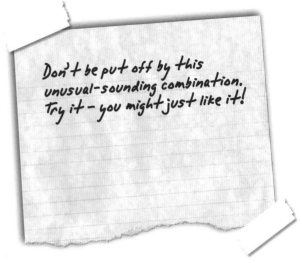

Don't be put off by this unusual-sounding combination. Try it - you might just like it!

Method

1 Beat the eggs with a fork and add the sugar.

2 Mix in the cornflakes briskly, so that they do not soften too much.

3 Melt the butter in a frying pan until it foams and then pour in the cornflake and egg mixture.

4 Cook for 4–5 minutes, stirring occasionally, until the eggs have set softly.

5 Transfer to a serving plate and sprinkle with a little extra sugar and a pinch of cinnamon.

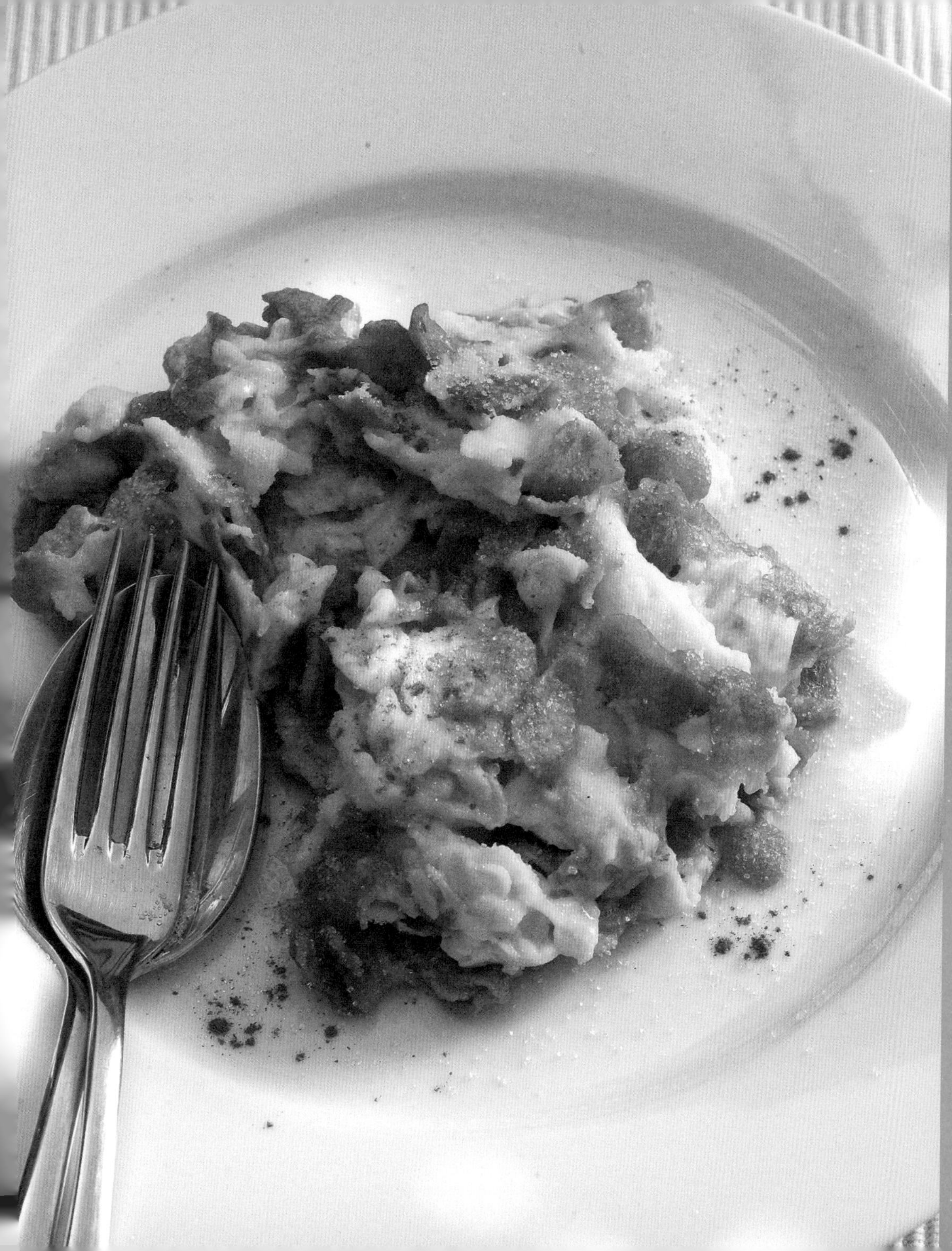

french toast

Serves 2

Ingredients

2 slices stale white bread

100 ml/3½ fl oz milk

1 egg

pinch of salt

2 tbsp unsalted butter

½ tsp ground cinnamon

1 tsp granulated sugar

Method

1 Slice the bread in half diagonally and place, in a single layer, in a shallow dish. Pour over the milk and leave to soak for 1–2 minutes, then turn over the bread.

2 Place the egg and salt in a bowl and beat well. Dip the soaked bread slices into the egg mix.

3 Heat the butter in a frying pan until it foams, then add the bread slices. Cook the French toast until golden brown on both sides. Drain on kitchen paper, then transfer to serving plates.

4 Mix together the cinnamon and sugar in a small bowl, then sprinkle over the French toast. Serve immediately.

cinnamon apples on fruit toast

Serves 1

Ingredients

1 tbsp unsalted butter

½ tsp ground cinnamon

1 apple, cored and sliced

1 slice fruit bread

golden syrup, to serve

Method

1 Melt the butter in a saucepan over a low heat and stir in the cinnamon. Add the apple and stir well to coat.

2 Preheat the grill and line the grill pan with foil. Spread the buttered apple over the grill pan. Cook under the grill until the apple is just beginning to brown.

3 Toast the fruit bread and serve with the apple piled on top, drizzled with a little golden syrup.

Fruity toast toppings make a tasty alternative to jam. A firm pear would work equally well in place of the apple.

apple pancakes with maple syrup butter

Serve 4–6

Ingredients
200 g/7 oz self-raising flour
100 g/3½ oz caster sugar
1 tsp ground cinnamon
1 egg
200 ml/7 fl oz milk
2 apples, peeled and grated
1 tsp butter
apple wedges, to serve

Maple syrup butter
85 g/3 oz butter, softened
3 tbsp maple syrup

> These pancakes are the perfect breakfast when you've got friends over to stay or if you fancy a pancake party! If your budget doesn't quite stretch to maple syrup, substitute golden syrup.

Method

1 Mix the flour, sugar and cinnamon together in a bowl and make a well in the centre. Beat the egg and the milk together and pour into the well. Using a wooden spoon, gently incorporate the dry ingredients into the liquid, then stir in the grated apple.

2 Melt the 1 teaspoon butter in a large non-stick frying pan over a low heat until melted and bubbling. Add tablespoons of the pancake mixture to form 9-cm/3½-inch circles. Cook each pancake for about 1 minute, until it starts to bubble lightly on the top and looks set, then flip it over and cook the other side for 30 seconds, or until cooked through. The pancakes should be golden brown; if not, increase the heat a little. Remove from the pan and keep warm. Repeat the process until all of the pancake batter has been used up.

3 To make the maple syrup butter, melt the 85 g/ 3 oz butter with the maple syrup in a saucepan over a low heat and stir until combined. To serve, place the pancakes on serving dishes and spoon over the flavoured butter. Serve warm with apple wedges.

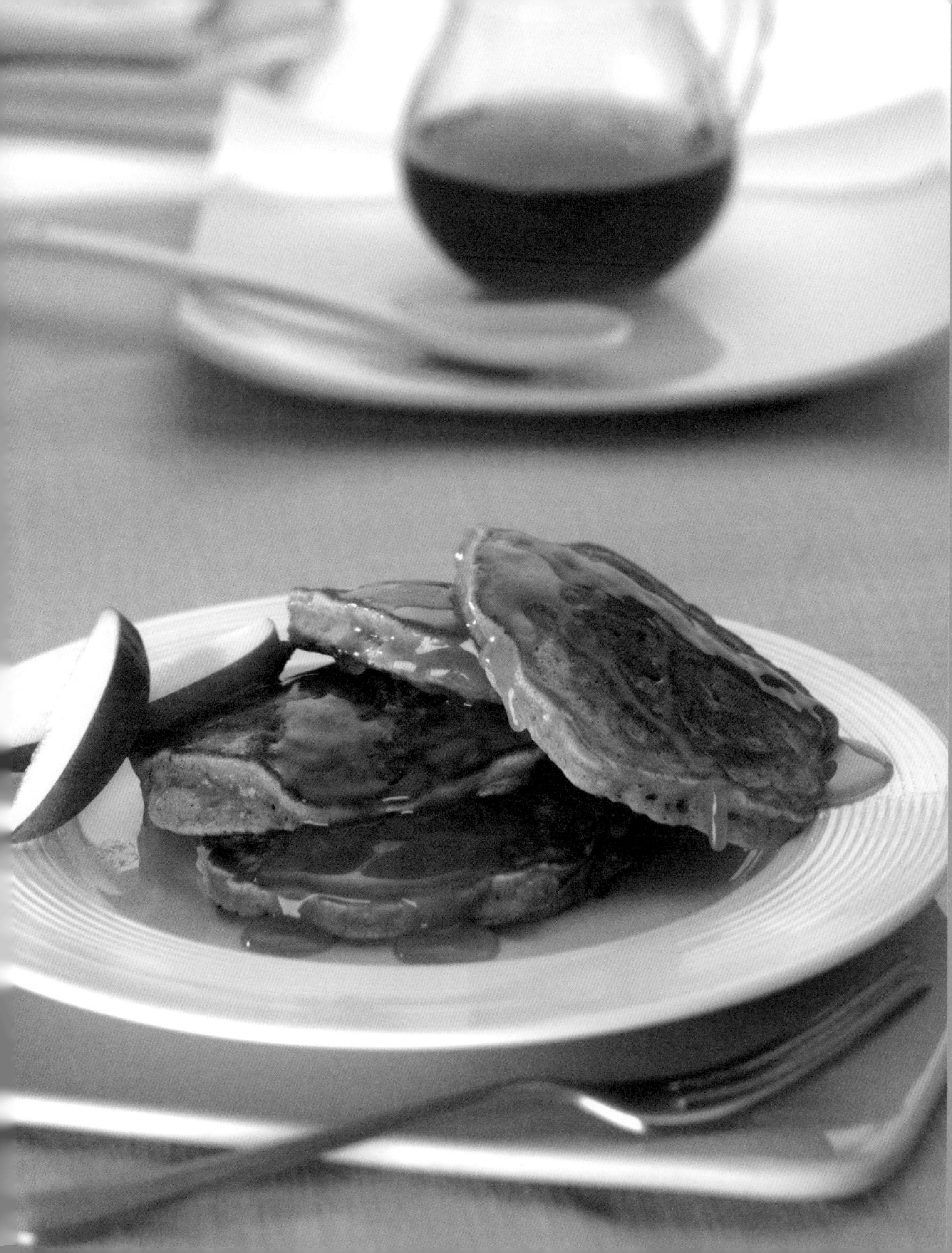

fruity muffins

Makes 10

Ingredients

280 g/10 oz self-raising wholemeal flour

2 tsp baking powder

2 tbsp dark muscovado sugar

100 g/3½ oz ready-to-eat dried apricots, finely chopped

1 banana, mashed with 1 tbsp orange juice

1 tsp finely grated orange rind

300 ml/10 fl oz milk

1 egg, beaten

3 tbsp sunflower oil

2 tbsp rolled oats

Baking is a great way to unwind and take your mind off your studies, and the delicious results are bound to make you popular with your housemates!

Method

1 Preheat the oven to 200°C/400°F/Gas Mark 6. Place 10 paper muffin cases in a muffin tin. Sift the flour and baking powder into a mixing bowl, adding any husks that remain in the sieve. Stir in the sugar and chopped apricots.

2 Make a well in the centre and add the banana, orange rind, milk, egg and oil. Stir gently to form a thick batter and divide among the muffin cases.

3 Sprinkle over the oats and bake in the preheated oven for 25–30 minutes, until well risen and firm to the touch or until a cocktail stick inserted into the centre comes out clean.

4 Remove the muffins from the oven and put them on a wire rack to cool slightly. Serve the muffins while still warm.

ham & cheese croissant

Serves 1

Ingredients

1 croissant

1 egg, hard-boiled and sliced (optional)

2 thin slices cooked ham, halved

mustard, to taste (optional)

2 slices hard cheese, such as Cheddar, Gruyère or Emmental (about 25 g/1 oz)

Method

1. Preheat the grill to medium–high. Slice the croissant horizontally in half, then lay it, cut-sides up, on the rack in the grill pan.

2. Top each croissant half with half the hard-boiled egg, if using, and a slice of ham, and spread with a little mustard, if using. Top with the cheese slices, cutting and overlapping them to fit the croissant. Grill for about 2 minutes, until the cheese has melted. The croissant will be warmed through and beginning to brown around the edges.

3. Use a knife to scoop any melted cheese off the foil and onto the croissant, then invert the top half on top of the bottom half. Serve immediately.

chive scrambled eggs

Serves 2

Ingredients

4 eggs

100 ml/3½ fl oz single cream

2 tbsp snipped fresh chives

25 g/1 oz butter

4 slices bread

salt and pepper

Method

1. Break the eggs into a medium bowl and whisk gently with the cream. Season to taste with salt and pepper and add the snipped chives.

2. Melt the butter in a frying pan and pour in the egg mixture. Leave to set slightly, then move the mixture towards the centre of the pan using a wooden spoon as the eggs begin to cook. Continue in this way until the eggs are cooked but still creamy.

3. Lightly toast the bread in a toaster or under the grill and place on plates. Spoon over the scrambled eggs and serve immediately.

For a hard-boiled egg, cook the egg in a saucepan of simmering water for 8 minutes.

sunshine toast

Serves 1

Ingredients

1 slice granary or wholemeal bread

1 tbsp olive oil

2–3 mushrooms, sliced

1 tomato, halved

1 small egg

pepper

Eggs are quick to cook and cheap to buy, making them the ultimate fast food. They can be cooked in so many different ways that you never need to get bored with eating them.

Method

1 Lightly toast the bread in the toaster or under a preheated grill. Using a biscuit cutter, cut a hole in the centre of the slice of toast, large enough to hold the egg.

2 Heat the oil in a non-stick frying pan and cook the mushrooms and tomato, cut-sides down, for 3–4 minutes, until the mushrooms are beginning to brown. Turn the tomato over.

3 Make a space in the middle of the pan and add the toast. Crack the egg open and carefully pour it into the hole in the toast. Reduce the heat and cook slowly until cooked through.

4 Season to taste with pepper, then transfer to a serving plate.

potato cakes with bacon & eggs

Serves 4

Ingredients
450 g/1 lb large potatoes, peeled

5 eggs

3 tbsp plain flour

3 tbsp sunflower oil

8 rashers bacon

6 cherry tomatoes, halved

salt and pepper

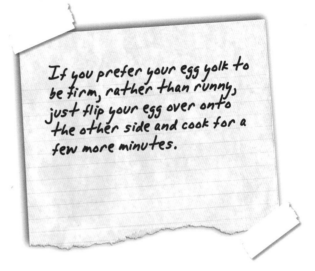

If you prefer your egg yolk to be firm, rather than runny, just flip your egg over onto the other side and cook for a few more minutes.

Method

1 Preheat the grill to medium–high.

2 Grate the potatoes, rinse in a colander, then spread out on a clean tea towel. Gather up the sides and squeeze to remove any water.

3 Beat 1 of the eggs in a large bowl. Add the potatoes, flour, and salt and pepper to taste and stir well. Take handfuls of the potato mixture and form into round patties about 7 cm/2¾ inches across. Heat 2 tablespoons of the oil in a frying pan. Cook the potato cakes, in batches, for 5 minutes on each side, until golden. Drain on paper towels.

4 Place the bacon on the grill rack and grill for 8 minutes, turning once, until crisp. Grill the tomatoes for 2–3 minutes.

5 Meanwhile, add the remaining oil to the frying pan and fry the remaining eggs for 5 minutes, until the white is set.

6 Transfer the potato cakes, bacon, tomatoes and eggs to plates and serve immediately.

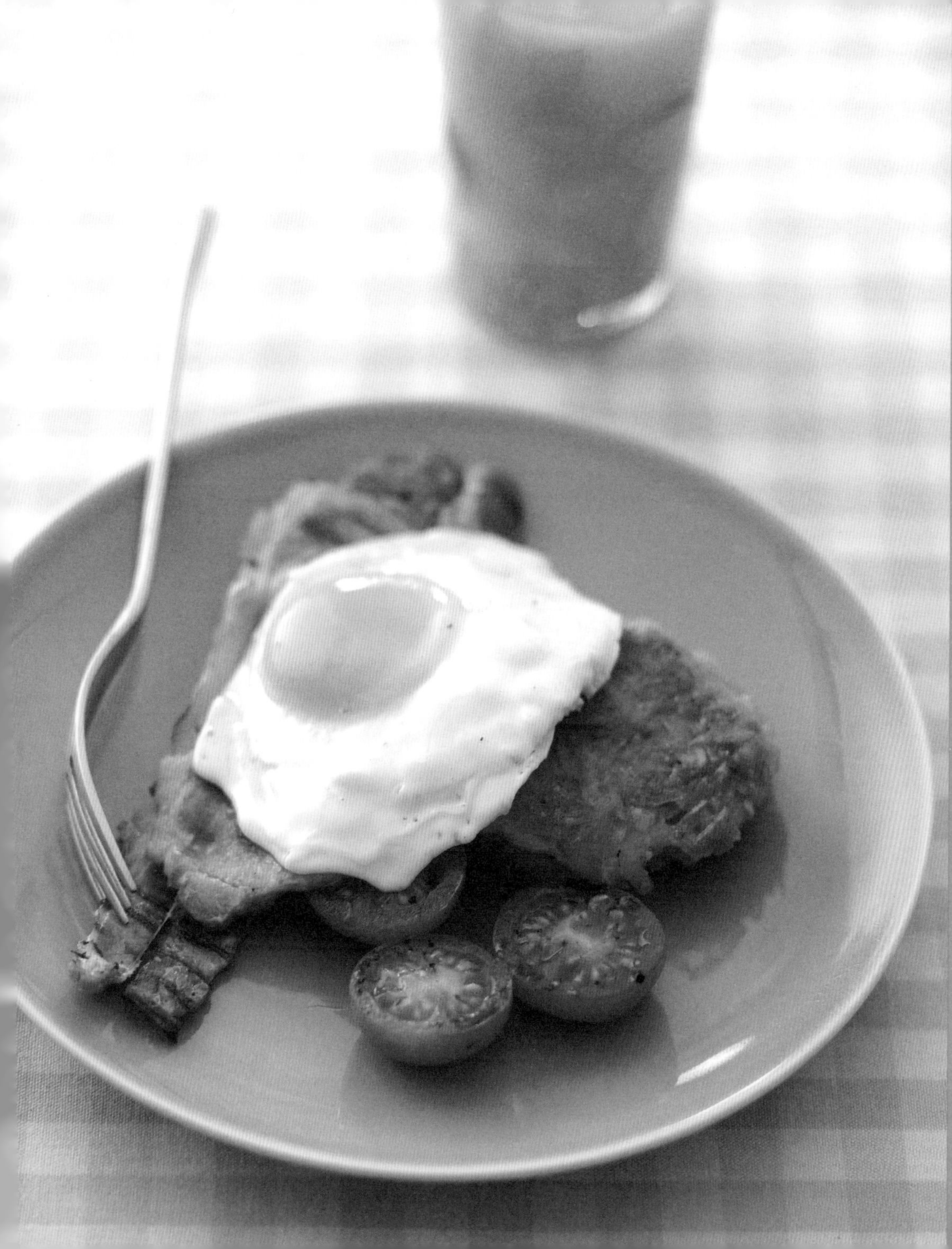

breakfast omelette

Serves 4

Ingredients

4 pork or vegetarian sausages

small knob of butter

2 tsp sunflower oil, plus extra if necessary

12 cherry tomatoes

6 eggs, beaten

salt and pepper

Method

1 Preheat the grill to medium–high. Line the grill pan with foil. Arrange the sausages on the grill rack and cook under the grill, turning frequently, until cooked through and golden all over. Leave to cool slightly, then cut into bite-sized pieces.

2 Meanwhile, melt the butter with the oil in a medium-sized frying pan with a heatproof handle and cook the tomatoes, turning occasionally, for 2 minutes.

3 Add the sausage pieces so that they are evenly distributed in the base of the frying pan among the tomatoes. Add a little more oil if the frying pan appears dry.

4 Season the eggs to taste with salt and pepper and pour over the sausages and tomatoes. Cook for 3 minutes, without stirring, then place the pan under the grill and cook the top for 3 minutes, or until set and lightly golden. Cut into wedges to serve.

baked eggs with ham & tomato

Serves 1

Ingredients

1 tsp olive oil

½ small leek, chopped

2 slices wafer-thin ham, chopped

1 egg

25 g/1 oz Cheddar cheese, grated

2 slices tomato

Method

1 Preheat the oven to 180°C/350°F/Gas Mark 4. Heat the oil in a saucepan and cook the leek for 5–6 minutes, until soft.

2 Place the leek in the bottom of a ramekin and top with the ham. Crack and pour in the egg, then top with the cheese and tomato.

3 Bake in the preheated oven for 10 minutes, until the egg is set. Remove the ramekin from the oven, leave to cool a little and serve.

To test whether an egg is fresh, place it in a bowl of water – generally, a stale egg will float.

eggs benedict

Serves 4

Ingredients
1 tbsp white wine vinegar

4 eggs

4 English muffins

4 slices ham

Quick hollandaise sauce
3 egg yolks, beaten

200 g/7 oz butter

1 tbsp lemon juice

pepper

> If you haven't got a blender or food processor, place the egg yolks in a heatproof bowl set over a saucepan of gently simmering water and gradually add the melted butter, beating constantly with a balloon whisk.

Method

1 To poach the eggs, fill a frying pan three-quarters full with water and bring to the boil over a low heat. Reduce the heat to a simmer and add the vinegar. When the water is barely simmering, carefully break the eggs into the frying pan. Poach the eggs for 3 minutes, or until the whites are just set but the yolks are still soft.

2 Meanwhile, to make the hollandaise sauce, place the egg yolks in a blender or food processor. Melt the butter in a small saucepan until bubbling. With the motor running, gradually add the hot butter to the blender in a steady stream until the sauce is thick and creamy. Add the lemon juice, and a little warm water if the sauce is too thick, then season to taste with pepper. Remove from the blender or food processor and keep warm.

3 Split the muffins and toast them on both sides. To serve, top each muffin with a slice of ham, a poached egg and a generous spoonful of hollandaise sauce.

grab
and go

The cost of buying lunch each day – even if it's only from a student canteen or refectory – can soon mount up. It might sound dull, but making your own is a great way to save cash. With plenty of inspiring ideas to choose from – including soups, salads and sweet treats – the recipes in this chapter prove that there is more to packed lunch than soggy sandwiches. Just prepare the night before and in the morning you can just grab…and go!

simply super sandwich fillings

Serves 2

Ingredients

Crunchy tuna
200 g/7 oz canned tuna,
  drained and flaked

1 tbsp canned sweetcorn, drained

1 tbsp chopped peppers

1 tbsp mayonnaise

Fruity cheese spread
100 g/3½ oz low-fat soft cheese

1 tbsp chopped stoned dates

2 tbsp chopped ready-to-eat dried apricots

Chicken & avocado
½ chicken breast, cooked and finely
  chopped

½ small avocado, mashed with
  2 tsp lemon juice

Making your own sandwiches is an easy way to save cash, but you'll quickly get bored with them if you have the same filling each day. Try these original ideas when you're short of inspiration.

Method
1 Mix the ingredients for each filling together and store in an airtight container in the refrigerator until required.

tex-mex roll-ups

Serves 2

Ingredients

2 corn tortillas

2 tbsp baked beans, mashed

2 tbsp grated Cheddar cheese

2–3 tbsp cooked chicken, finely chopped or shredded

1 tomato, sliced

¼ avocado, peeled and cut into strips

Method

1 Put each tortilla on a microwavable plate. Spread the beans over each tortilla and sprinkle with the cheese. Microwave for about 15 seconds until the cheese melts. Leave to cool slightly.

2 Arrange the chicken, tomato and avocado on top. Roll up and cut into small pieces. Wrap in foil for a packed lunch.

tortillas with tuna, egg & sweetcorn

Serves 2

Ingredients

1 tbsp natural yogurt

1 tsp olive oil

½ tsp white wine vinegar

½ tsp Dijon mustard

1 large egg, hard-boiled and cooled

200 g/7 oz canned tuna, drained

200 g/7 oz canned sweetcorn kernels, drained

2 flour tortillas

1 punnet mustard cress

pepper

Method

1 To make the dressing, whisk the yogurt, oil, vinegar, mustard and pepper to taste in a jug until emulsified and smooth.

2 Shell the egg, separate the yolk and the white, then mash the yolk and chop the white finely. Mash the tuna with the egg and dressing, then mix in the sweetcorn.

3 Spread the filling equally over the 2 tortillas and sprinkle over the mustard cress. Fold in one end and roll up. Wrap in foil for a packed lunch.

chicken wraps

Serves 4

Ingredients

150 g/5½ oz natural yogurt

1 tbsp wholegrain mustard

280 g/10 oz cooked chicken breast, diced

140 g/5 oz iceberg lettuce, finely shredded

85 g/3 oz cucumber, thinly sliced

2 celery sticks, sliced

85 g/3 oz black seedless grapes, halved

4 flour tortillas

pepper

Method

1 Combine the yogurt and mustard in a bowl and season to taste with pepper. Stir in the chicken and toss until thoroughly coated.

2 Put the lettuce, cucumber, celery and grapes into a separate bowl and mix well.

3 Fold a tortilla in half and in half again to make a cone that is easy to hold. Half-fill the tortilla pocket with the salad mixture and top with some of the chicken mixture. Repeat with the remaining tortillas, salad and chicken. Wrap in foil for a packed lunch.

turkey salad pitta

Makes 1

Ingredients

small handful baby leaf spinach, rinsed, patted dry and shredded

½ red pepper, deseeded and thinly sliced

½ carrot, peeled and coarsely grated

4 tbsp hummus

85 g/3 oz cooked turkey, thinly sliced

½ tbsp sunflower seeds

1 wholemeal pitta bread

salt and pepper

Method

1 Preheat the grill to high.

2 Put the spinach leaves, red pepper, carrot and hummus into a large bowl and stir together, so all the salad ingredients are coated with the hummus. Stir in the turkey and sunflower seeds and season to taste with salt and pepper.

3 Put the pitta bread under the grill for about 1 minute on each side to warm through, but do not brown. Cut it in half to make 2 'pockets' of bread.

4 Divide the filling between the bread pockets. Wrap in foil for a packed lunch.

creamy tomato soup

Serves 4–6

Ingredients

15 g/½ oz butter

½ red onion, finely chopped

1 leek, chopped

1 garlic clove, crushed

1 carrot, peeled and grated

1 potato, peeled and grated

300 ml/10 fl oz vegetable stock

500 g/1 lb 2 oz ripe tomatoes, peeled,
    deseeded and chopped

1 tbsp tomato purée

150 ml/5 fl oz full-fat milk

salt and pepper

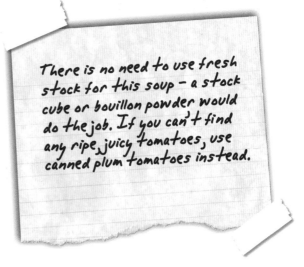

There is no need to use fresh stock for this soup – a stock cube or bouillon powder would do the job. If you can't find any ripe, juicy tomatoes, use canned plum tomatoes instead.

Method

1 Melt the butter in a large saucepan over a low heat and cook the onion, leek and garlic for 10 minutes, or until very soft but not browned.

2 Add the carrot and potato and cook for 5 minutes. Add the stock and bring up to simmering point.

3 Add the tomatoes and tomato purée and season to taste with salt and pepper. Simmer for 15 minutes, until the vegetables are very soft. Add the milk and warm through, then liquidize the soup in the saucepan using a hand-held stick blender. You can pass the soup through a sieve at this stage, if you like.

4 Ladle the soup into serving bowls or transfer to a flask for a packed lunch.

leek & potato soup

Serves 4–6

Ingredients

55 g/2 oz butter

1 onion, chopped

3 leeks, sliced

225 g/8 oz potatoes, peeled and cut into 2-cm/¾-inch cubes

850 ml/1½ pints vegetable stock

150 ml/5 fl oz single cream (optional)

salt and pepper

fresh flat-leaf parsley sprigs, to garnish (optional)

Method

1 Melt the butter in a large saucepan over a medium heat, add the onion, leeks and potatoes and sauté gently for 2–3 minutes, until soft but not brown. Pour in the stock, bring to the boil, then reduce the heat and simmer, covered, for 15 minutes.

2 Remove from the heat and liquidize the soup in the saucepan using a hand-held stick blender.

3 Heat the soup, season to taste with salt and pepper and transfer to serving bowls. Swirl with the cream and garnish with parsley sprigs, if using. Alternatively, transfer to a flask for a packed lunch.

chicken noodle soup

Serves 4

Ingredients

2 skinless, boneless chicken breasts

1.2 litres/2 pints water or chicken stock

3 carrots, peeled and cut into 5-mm/¼-inch slices

85 g/3 oz vermicelli (or other fine noodles)

salt and pepper

1 tbsp fresh tarragon leaves (optional)

Method

1 Place the chicken breasts in a large saucepan, add the water and bring to a simmer. Cook for 25–30 minutes. Skim any scum from the surface if necessary. Remove the chicken from the water and keep warm.

2 Continue to simmer, add the carrots and vermicelli and cook for 4–5 minutes.

3 Thinly slice or shred the chicken breasts and place in serving bowls.

4 Season the soup to taste with salt and pepper. Pour over the chicken and scatter with the tarragon leaves, if using. Alternatively, stir the chicken and tarragon, if using, into the soup and transfer to a flask for a packed lunch.

Store any leftover soup in an airtight container in the fridge, or freeze for another day.

spicy red lentil soup

Serves 4

Ingredients

300 g/10½ oz red lentils, picked
    over and rinsed

2 litres/3½ pints vegetable stock or water

2 green chillies, split

1 tsp turmeric

2 tbsp sunflower oil

1½ onions, thinly sliced

2 large garlic cloves, crushed

2 tsp curry paste, mild, medium or hot,
    to taste

salt and pepper

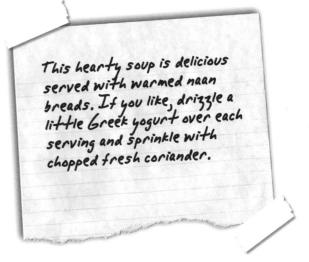

This hearty soup is delicious served with warmed naan breads. If you like, drizzle a little Greek yogurt over each serving and sprinkle with chopped fresh coriander.

Method

1 Put the lentils and stock into a large saucepan with a tight-fitting lid. Place over a high heat and slowly bring to the boil, skimming the surface as necessary. Add the chillies and turmeric, reduce the heat to very low, cover the pan and leave the lentils to simmer for 25–30 minutes, until they are very soft and mushy.

2 Meanwhile, heat the oil in another large saucepan over a medium heat. Add the onions and garlic and fry for 5–7 minutes, until the onions are tender but not brown. Add the curry paste and cook, stirring, for about a minute.

3 Liquidize the soup in the saucepan using a hand-held stick blender. Add enough water to reach the desired consistency and slowly bring to the boil, then reduce the heat and simmer for 2 minutes. Season to taste with salt and pepper.

4 Ladle the soup into serving bowls or transfer to a flask for a packed lunch.

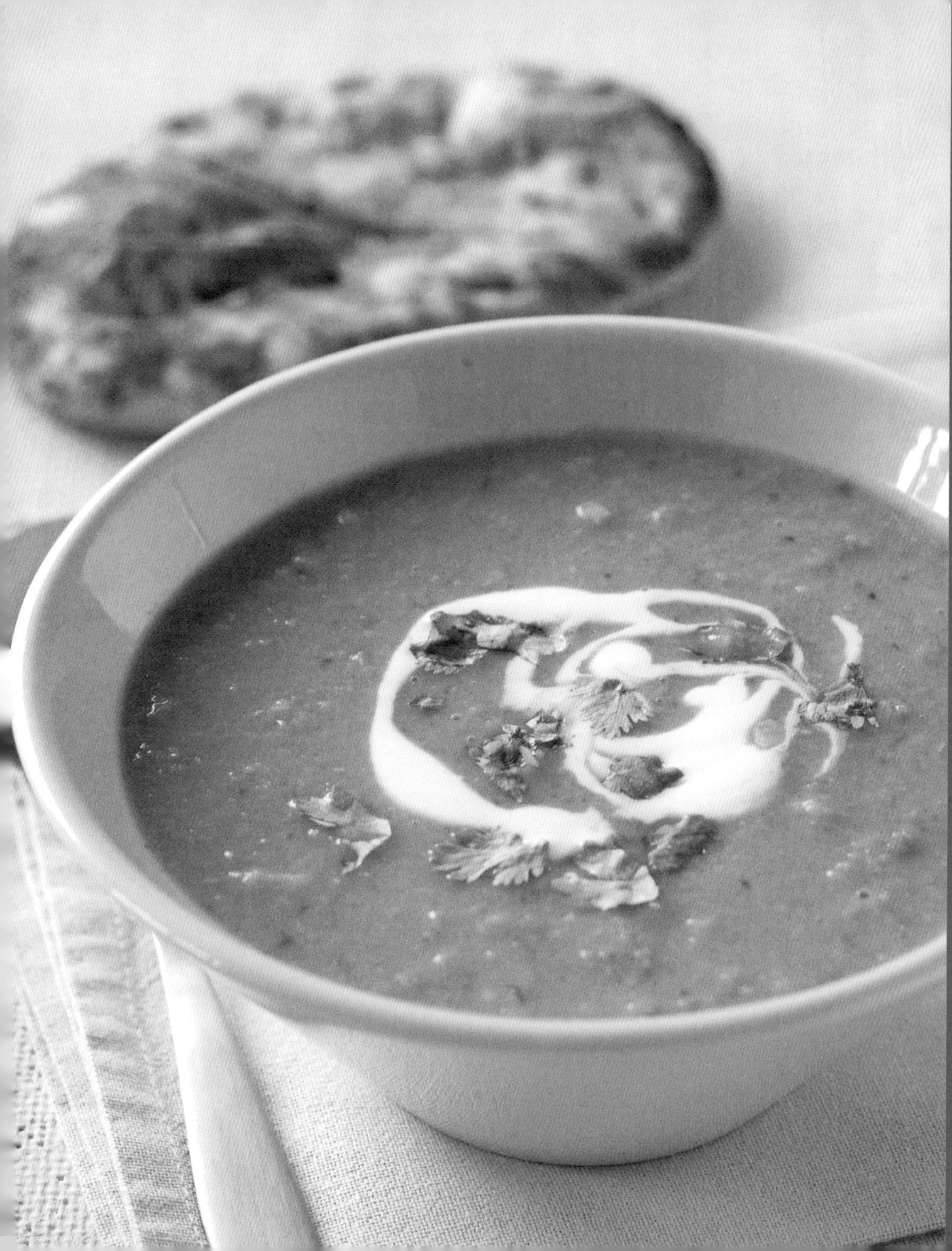

spanish omelette

Serves 2

Ingredients

200 g/7 oz new potatoes

1 tbsp olive oil

1 onion, thinly sliced

1 red pepper, deseeded and thinly sliced

2 tomatoes, peeled, deseeded and chopped

6 large eggs

1 tbsp milk

2 tbsp finely grated Parmesan cheese

salt and pepper

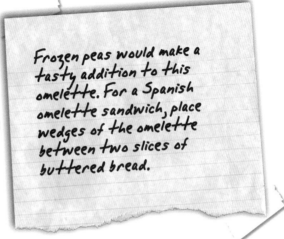

Frozen peas would make a tasty addition to this omelette. For a Spanish omelette sandwich, place wedges of the omelette between two slices of buttered bread.

Method

1 Cook the potatoes in a saucepan of boiling water for 8–12 minutes, until tender. Drain and leave to cool, then slice.

2 Heat the oil in an 18–20-cm/7–8-inch frying pan with a heatproof handle and cook the onion and red pepper until soft. Add the tomatoes and cook for a further minute.

3 Add the potatoes to the pan and spread out evenly.

4 Beat the eggs, milk and cheese, with salt and pepper to taste, in a bowl and pour over the potato mixture. Cook for 4–5 minutes, until the eggs are set underneath.

5 Meanwhile, preheat the grill to high. Place the frying pan under the grill and cook the omelette for a further 3–4 minutes, until the eggs are set.

6 Leave to cool, then cut into wedges and wrap in foil for a packed lunch.

cheesy sweetcorn fritters

Serves 2

Ingredients

1 egg

200 ml/7 fl oz milk

100 g/3½ oz plain flour

½ tsp baking powder

85 g/3 oz canned sweetcorn kernels, drained

4 tbsp grated Cheddar cheese

1 tsp snipped fresh chives

2 tsp sunflower oil

For a healthy lunch, serve the sweetcorn fritters with extra sweetcorn and carrot sticks on the side.

Method

1 Put the egg and milk into a small bowl and beat with a fork. Add the flour and baking powder and beat until smooth. Stir in the sweetcorn, cheese and chives.

2 Heat the oil in a frying pan and drop either teaspoonfuls or tablespoonfuls of the batter into it. Cook for 1–2 minutes on each side, until the fritters are puffed up and golden.

3 Drain on kitchen paper and serve immediately or leave to cool and wrap in foil for a packed lunch.

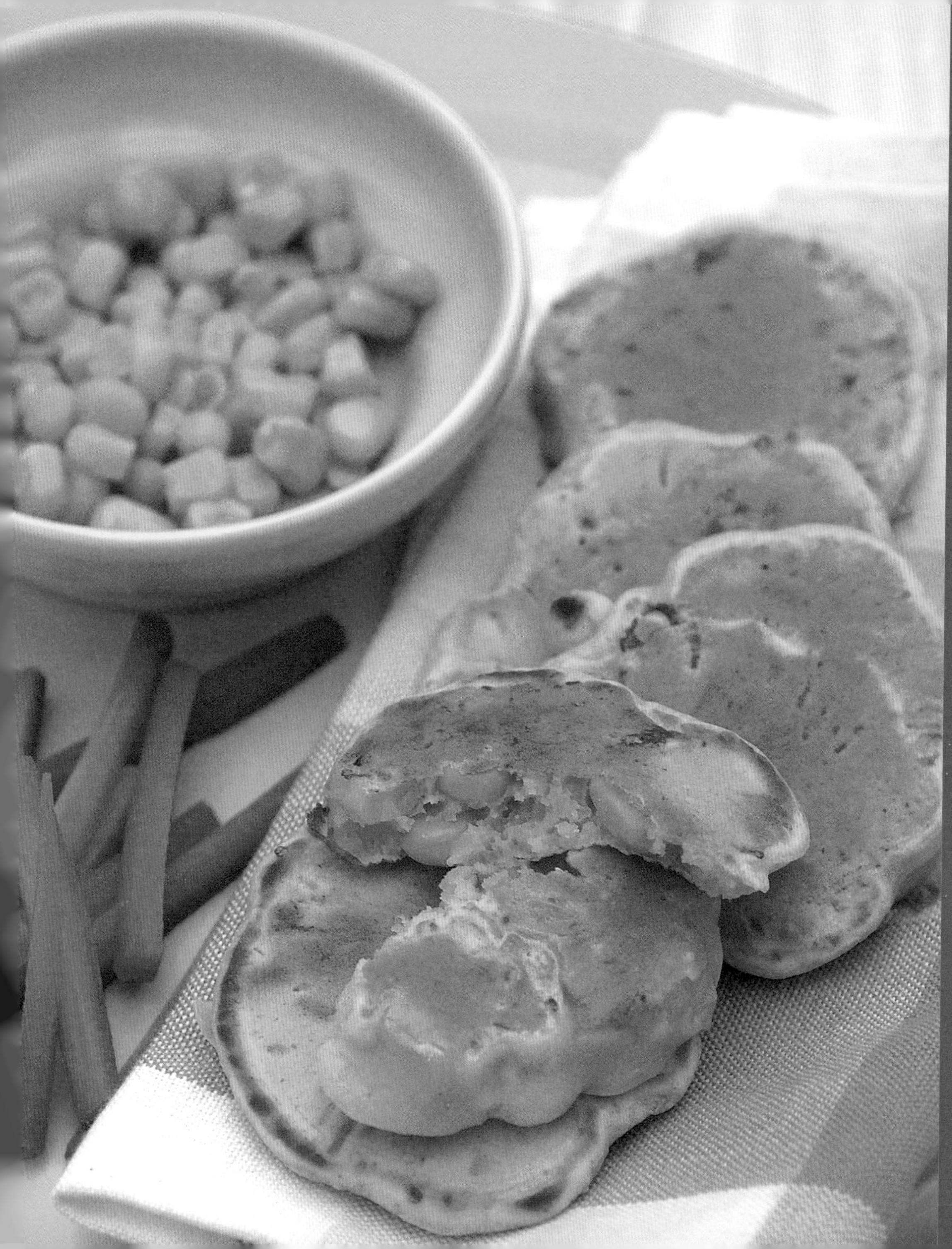

bread, onion & tomato salad

Serves 2

Ingredients

2–3 bread rolls, depending on size

3 tbsp white wine vinegar

5 tbsp extra virgin olive oil

6 slices salami

1 tomato

1 large onion

1 spring onion

salt and pepper

Method

1 Break the bread rolls into pieces and place in a bowl. Pour over the vinegar and oil and leave to stand for 10 minutes, stirring frequently.

2 Chop up the salami and the tomato.

3 Peel the onion, halve it and cut into slices lengthways.

4 Add all of the chopped ingredients to the bread mixture. Season to taste with salt and pepper.

5 Mix together carefully. Finely chop the spring onion and scatter over the salad before serving. Transfer to an airtight container for a packed lunch.

roasted vegetable salad

Serves 4

Ingredients

1 onion

1 aubergine

1 red pepper, deseeded

1 orange pepper, deseeded

1 large courgette

2–4 garlic cloves

2–4 tbsp olive oil

1 tbsp balsamic vinegar

2 tbsp extra virgin olive oil

1 tbsp shredded fresh basil

salt and pepper

Parmesan cheese shavings, to serve

Method

1 Preheat the oven to 200°C/400°F/Gas Mark 6. Cut all the vegetables into even-sized wedges, put into a roasting tin and scatter over the garlic. Pour over 2 tablespoons of the olive oil and toss the vegetables until well coated. Season to taste with salt and pepper. Roast in the preheated oven for 40 minutes, or until tender, adding the extra olive oil if needed.

2 Meanwhile, put the vinegar, extra virgin olive oil and salt and pepper to taste into a screw-top jar and shake until blended.

3 Once the vegetables are cooked, remove from the oven, arrange on a serving dish and pour over the dressing. Sprinkle with the basil and serve with Parmesan cheese shavings. Transfer to an airtight container for a packed lunch.

Salads are great for a packed lunch — store in a mini cool bag to keep them fresh until lunchtime.

pasta salad

Serves 2

Ingredients

100 g/3½ oz dried pasta shapes

1 tbsp olive oil, plus extra if needed

1 tbsp mayonnaise

1 tbsp natural yogurt

2 tbsp pesto

200 g/7 oz canned tuna, drained and flaked

200 g/7 oz canned sweetcorn kernels, drained

2 tomatoes, peeled, deseeded and chopped

½ green pepper, deseeded and chopped

½ avocado, stoned, peeled and chopped

salt and pepper

Pasta salads are incredibly versatile – just add any salad ingredients you have to hand. Vegetarians could use drained canned beans in place of the tuna.

Method

1 Cook the pasta in a large saucepan of boiling water for 8–10 minutes, until just tender. Drain, return to the saucepan and add the oil. Toss well to coat, then cover and leave to cool.

2 To make the dressing, whisk the mayonnaise, yogurt and pesto together in a jug, adding a little oil if needed to achieve the desired consistency. Add a pinch of salt and season to taste with pepper.

3 Mix the cooled pasta with the tuna, sweetcorn, tomatoes, green pepper and avocado, add the dressing and toss well to coat. Transfer to an airtight container for a packed lunch.

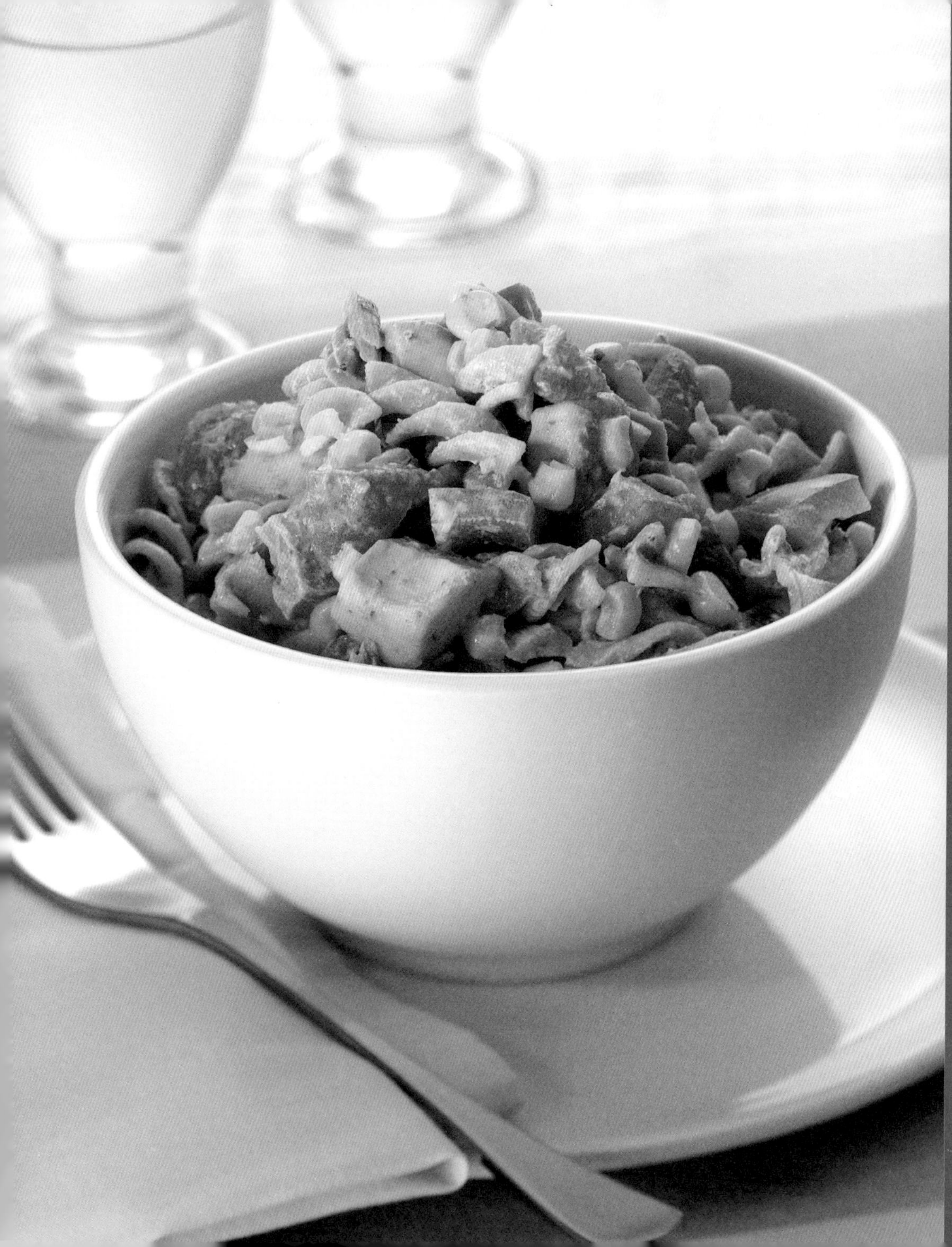

rice salad

Serves 2

Ingredients

1 leek

1 red pepper

160 g/5¾ oz canned sweetcorn

300 g/10½ oz cooked long-grain rice

5 basil leaves

3 tbsp white wine vinegar

2 tbsp olive oil

salt and pepper

Method

1 Slice the leek into thin rings.

2 Wash the red pepper, deseed and chop into 1-cm/
½-inch cubes. Drain the sweetcorn.

3 Add the chopped pepper, chopped leek and the
sweetcorn to the rice in a bowl. Slice the basil
leaves into strips and put them into the bowl.

4 Mix together the vinegar and oil in a small bowl,
then season to taste with salt and pepper and pour
over the rice salad.

5 Mix everything together well. Transfer to an airtight
container for a packed lunch.

tabbouleh

Serves 4

Ingredients

175 g/6 oz bulgar wheat

3 tbsp extra virgin olive oil

4 tbsp lemon juice

4 spring onions

1 green pepper, deseeded and sliced

4 tomatoes, chopped

2 tbsp chopped fresh parsley

2 tbsp chopped fresh mint

8 black olives, stoned

salt and pepper

Method

1 Place the bulgar wheat in a large bowl and add
enough cold water to cover. Leave to stand for
30 minutes, or until doubled in size. Drain well and
press out as much liquid as possible. Spread out
the wheat on kitchen paper to dry.

2 Place the wheat in a serving bowl. Mix the oil and
lemon juice together in a jug and season to taste
with salt and pepper. Pour over the wheat and
leave to marinate for 1 hour.

3 Using a sharp knife, finely chop the spring onions,
then add to the salad with the green pepper,
tomatoes, parsley and mint and toss lightly to mix.
Top the salad with the olives. Transfer to an airtight
container for a packed lunch.

Save money by keeping pots
of fresh herbs on your
windowsill to use each time
you cook.

barbecue chicken

Serves 4

Ingredients
4 chicken drumsticks, about 100 g/3½ oz
each, skinned

Barbecue sauce
1 shallot, finely chopped

1 garlic clove, crushed

1 tbsp tomato purée blended with
150 ml/5 fl oz water

2 tbsp red wine vinegar

1 tbsp prepared mustard

1 tbsp Worcestershire sauce

These piquant chicken drumsticks are equally delicious served hot or cold. Chicken drumsticks are much cheaper than chicken breasts, although you could use either for this recipe.

Method

1 To make the barbecue sauce, place the shallot, garlic, tomato purée mixture, vinegar, mustard and Worcestershire sauce in a screw-top jar, cover with the lid and shake vigorously until well blended.

2 Rinse the chicken drumsticks and pat dry with kitchen paper. Place the drumsticks in a large ovenproof dish, pour over the sauce and leave to stand for at least 2 hours, occasionally spooning the sauce over the chicken.

3 Preheat the oven to 190°C/375°F/Gas Mark 5. Cook the chicken drumsticks in the oven for 20–25 minutes, or until the juices run clear when a skewer is inserted into the thickest part of the meat. Spoon the sauce over the chicken or turn the chicken over during cooking.

4 Serve immediately or leave to cool and chill in the refrigerator until ready to serve.

mini savoury pies

Makes 6

Ingredients

butter, for greasing

200 g/7 oz ready-rolled puff pastry, thawed if frozen

plain flour, for dusting

3 eggs, beaten

125 ml/4 fl oz milk

85 g/3 oz mature Cheddar cheese, grated

1 slice ham, chopped (optional)

1 tomato, sliced

salt and pepper

Method

1 Preheat the oven to 200°C/400°F/Gas Mark 6. Grease a deep 6-hole muffin tin.

2 Roll the pastry out on a lightly floured work surface until it is very thin. Cut out 6 rounds to fit the size of the muffin hole, making sure that the pastry extends just above the rim of the hole.

3 Whisk the eggs and milk together in a bowl and season to taste with salt and pepper. Divide the cheese between the pastry cases. Sprinkle with ham, if using, then pour the egg mixture over the top. Top each pie with a tomato slice.

4 Bake in the preheated oven for 20–25 minutes, or until risen and golden. Leave to cool slightly before removing the pies from the tin.

cheese twists

Serves 4–6

Ingredients

butter, for greasing

85 g/3 oz Gruyère cheese, grated

½ tsp paprika

375 g/13 oz ready-rolled puff pastry, thawed if frozen

1 egg, beaten

Method

1 Preheat the oven to 200°C/400°F/Gas Mark 6. Grease a large baking sheet.

2 Mix together the cheese and paprika and sprinkle over the sheet of puff pastry. Fold the puff pastry in half and roll out a little to seal the edges.

3 Cut the pastry into long 1-cm/½-inch wide strips, then cut each strip in half and gently twist. Place on the prepared baking sheet. Brush with the beaten egg and bake in the preheated oven for 10–12 minutes, or until crisp and golden. Place on a wire rack and leave to cool.

Making fresh puff pastry is incredibly fiddly and time-consuming so it's really worth splashing out on ready-made pastry.

banana loaf

Serves 8

Ingredients

butter, for greasing
125 g/4½ oz white self-raising flour
100 g/3½ oz light brown self-raising flour
150 g/5½ oz demerara sugar
pinch of salt
½ tsp ground cinnamon
½ tsp ground nutmeg
2 large ripe bananas, peeled
175 ml/6 fl oz orange juice
2 eggs, beaten
4 tbsp sunflower oil

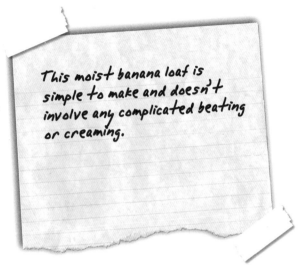

This moist banana loaf is simple to make and doesn't involve any complicated beating or creaming.

Method

1 Preheat the oven to 180°C/350°F/Gas Mark 4. Lightly grease and line a 900-g/2-lb loaf tin.

2 Sift the flours, sugar, salt and the spices into a large bowl. In a separate bowl mash the bananas with the orange juice, then stir in the eggs and oil. Pour into the dry ingredients and mix well.

3 Spoon into the prepared tin and bake in the preheated oven for 1 hour. Test to see if the loaf is cooked by inserting a skewer into the centre. If it comes out clean, the loaf is done. If not, bake for a further 10 minutes and test again.

4 Remove from the oven and leave to cool in the tin. Turn out the loaf, slice and serve.

peanut butter cookies

Makes 26

Ingredients

115 g/4 oz butter, softened,
    plus extra for greasing
115 g/4 oz crunchy peanut butter
115 g/4 oz caster sugar
115 g/4 oz light muscovado sugar
1 egg, beaten
½ tsp vanilla essence
85 g/3 oz plain flour
½ tsp bicarbonate of soda
½ tsp baking powder
pinch of salt
115 g/4 oz rolled oats

Nothing beats this cookie classic with its curious but compelling combination of sweet and salty flavours. Try this recipe and see for yourself!

Method

1 Preheat the oven to 180°C/350°F/Gas Mark 4. Grease a large baking tray.

2 Place the butter and peanut butter in a bowl and beat together. Beat in the caster sugar and muscovado sugar, then gradually beat in the egg and the vanilla essence.

3 Sift the flour, bicarbonate of soda, baking powder and salt into the mixture, add the oats and stir until just combined.

4 Place spoonfuls of the mixture onto the prepared baking trays, spaced well apart to allow for spreading. Flatten slightly with a fork.

5 Bake in the preheated oven for 12 minutes, or until lightly browned. Leave to cool on the baking tray for 2 minutes, then transfer to a wire rack to cool completely.

orange flapjack fingers

Makes 18

Ingredients

175 g/6 oz butter, plus extra for greasing

150 g/5½ oz golden syrup

70 g/2½ oz demerara sugar

200 g/7 oz rolled oats

70 g/2½ oz plain wholemeal flour

70 g/2½ oz raisins or sultanas

finely grated rind of 1 large orange

Method

1 Preheat the oven to 180°C/375°F/Gas Mark 4. Grease a shallow 25 x 20-cm/10 x 8-inch baking tin, then line with baking paper.

2 Put the butter, golden syrup and sugar into a saucepan over a high heat and stir until the butter and syrup have melted and the sugar has dissolved, then bring to the boil without stirring.

3 Put the oats, flour, raisins and orange rind into a large heatproof bowl. Pour in the butter mixture and mix all the ingredients together. Tip into the prepared tin and use the back of a wooden spoon to spread evenly over the base of the tin and into the corners.

4 Bake in the preheated oven for 25–30 minutes, until the flapjack mixture has set. Remove from the oven, place on a wire rack and leave to cool completely. When cool, cut into fingers.

no-bake chocolate cake

Serves 6–8

Ingredients

225 g/8 oz plain chocolate

225 g/8 oz unsalted butter

3 tbsp black coffee

55 g/2 oz light brown sugar

few drops of vanilla essence

225 g/8 oz digestive biscuits, crushed

85 g/3 oz raisins

85 g/3 oz walnuts, chopped

Method

1 Line a 450-g/1-lb loaf tin with baking paper. Melt the chocolate, butter, coffee, sugar and vanilla essence in a saucepan over a low heat.

2 Stir in the crushed biscuits, raisins and walnuts and stir well.

3 Spoon the mixture into the prepared loaf tin.

4 Leave to set for 1–2 hours in the refrigerator, then turn out and cut into thin slices to serve.

These tasty treats are perfect mid-morning or afternoon snacks. Store in an airtight container for up to 1 week – if they last that long!

simple
suppers

There's nothing worse than getting home in the evening and not having a clue what to cook. You're hungry and your brain is so frazzled that just thinking about dinner makes your head hurt! That's where this chapter comes in with its selection of supper solutions. The recipes are so straightforward that even novice cooks can't fail to be impressed. What's more, many are super speedy and can be on your plate within half an hour.

baked chilli cheese sandwiches

Makes 4

Ingredients

350 g/12 oz grated cheese, such as Cheddar

150 g/5½ oz butter, softened, plus extra to finish

4 fresh green chillies, deseeded and chopped

½ tsp ground cumin

8 thick slices bread

Method

1 Preheat the oven to 190°C/375°F/Gas Mark 5. Mix the cheese and 115 g/4 oz of the butter together in a bowl until combined, then add the chillies and cumin.

2 Use the remaining butter to spread over one side of each slice of bread. Place 4 slices, butter-side down, on a baking sheet, then spread the cheese mixture over the top. Top with the remaining slices of bread, butter-side up and press down.

3 Bake in the preheated oven for 8–10 minutes, until crisp and lightly browned. Serve.

mini muffin pizzas

Makes 6

Ingredients

3 wholemeal English muffins, halved

2 tbsp tomato purée

2 tbsp pesto

1 tbsp olive oil

½ red onion, thinly sliced

3 mushrooms, sliced

½ courgette, thinly sliced

2–3 slices ham or 6 slices salami

100 g/3½ oz grated Cheddar cheese or 6 slices mozzarella cheese

Method

1 Preheat the grill to high. Toast the muffins until golden, then leave to cool.

2 Mix the tomato purée and pesto together in a small bowl and spread equally over the muffin halves.

3 Heat the oil in a non-stick frying pan and then cook the onion, mushrooms and courgette until soft and beginning to brown.

4 Divide the vegetables between the muffins and top with the ham and then the cheese.

5 Cook under the grill for 3–4 minutes, until the cheese is melted and browned. Serve hot or cold.

The chilli cheese sandwiches can be cooked in a sandwich toaster, if you have one.

italian steak sandwiches

Serves 4

Ingredients

1 tbsp olive oil, plus extra for brushing

1 small onion, finely chopped

1 garlic clove, finely chopped

1 small red pepper, deseeded and finely chopped

100 g/3½ oz button mushrooms, finely chopped

200 g/7 oz fresh beef steak mince

125 ml/4 fl oz red wine

2 tbsp tomato purée

4 bread rolls

75 g/2¾ oz mozzarella cheese

2 tbsp torn fresh basil leaves

salt and pepper

These sandwiches taste better if you leave them to stand and allow the delicious flavours to develop. However, you can eat them straight away if you're short of time.

Method

1 Heat the oil in a large saucepan over a medium heat, add the onion, garlic, pepper and mushrooms and cook, stirring occasionally, for 5–10 minutes, until softened and beginning to brown.

2 Add the mince and cook, stirring frequently and breaking up any lumps with a wooden spoon, for 5 minutes, or until well browned. Add the wine, tomato purée and salt and pepper to taste and leave to simmer for 10 minutes, stirring occasionally. Remove from the heat.

3 Split the bread rolls in half and brush both halves with oil. Put the bottom halves onto a piece of foil and spoon an equal quantity of the sauce on top of each.

4 Slice the cheese, then divide between the roll bottoms and arrange on top of the sauce. Add the basil leaves and cover with the tops of the rolls. Press down gently and wrap in the foil. Leave the sandwiches for at least 1 hour before serving.

mushroom fajitas

Serves 4–8

Ingredients

500 g/1 lb 2 oz large flat mushrooms

2 tbsp oil

1 onion, sliced

1 red pepper, deseeded and sliced

1 green pepper, deseeded and sliced

1 garlic clove, crushed

¼–½ tsp cayenne pepper

juice and grated rind of 2 limes

2 tsp sugar

1 tsp dried oregano

8 flour tortillas

salt and pepper

Method

1 Cut the mushrooms into strips. Heat the oil in a large heavy-based frying pan. Add the mushrooms, onion, red and green peppers and garlic and stir-fry for 8–10 minutes, until the vegetables are cooked.

2 Add the cayenne pepper, lime juice and rind, sugar and oregano. Season to taste with salt and pepper and cook for a further 2 minutes.

3 Meanwhile, heat the tortillas according to the packet instructions. Divide the mushroom mixture between the warmed tortillas and serve.

chorizo & cheese quesadillas

Serves 4–8

Ingredients

115 g/4 oz mozzarella cheese, grated

115 g/4 oz Cheddar cheese, grated

225 g/8 oz chorizo sausage (outer casing removed) or ham, diced

4 spring onions, finely chopped

2 fresh green chillies, deseeded and finely chopped

8 flour tortillas

vegetable oil, for brushing

salt and pepper

Method

1 Place the cheeses, chorizo, spring onions, chillies and salt and pepper to taste in a bowl and mix together.

2 Divide the mixture between 4 of the flour tortillas, then top with the remaining tortillas.

3 Brush a large heavy-based frying pan with oil and heat over a medium heat. Add 1 quesadilla and cook, pressing it down with a spatula, for 4–5 minutes, until the underside is crisp and lightly browned. Turn over and cook the other side until the cheese has melted. Remove from the frying pan and keep warm. Cook the remaining quesadillas.

4 Cut each quesadilla into quarters, arrange on a warmed serving plate and serve.

These Mexican favourites are great for chilled-out nights in with a bunch of mates and a DVD. Serve with soured cream, salsa and guacamole.

chinese rice with omelette strips

Serves 2

Ingredients

2 tsp vegetable oil

a few drops of sesame oil (optional)

1 small garlic clove, finely chopped

pinch of Chinese five-spice powder

1 carrot, peeled and diced

2 baby corn, halved and thinly sliced

small handful of baby spinach, tough stems removed and finely sliced

175 g/6 oz cooked brown or white rice

dash of soy sauce

1 tsp sesame seeds (optional)

small knob of unsalted butter

1 egg, beaten

This recipe turns leftover rice into a tasty and filling meal. Make sure to store cooked rice in the refrigerator and use within 1-2 days.

Method

1 Heat the vegetable oil and sesame oil, if using, in a wok or heavy-based frying pan. Add the garlic, five spice, carrot and baby corn and stir-fry for 5 minutes, stirring and tossing constantly to prevent the spices and vegetables burning and sticking.

2 Add 2 tablespoons of water and stir-fry for 2 minutes, then mix in the spinach and cook, stirring frequently, for a further 2 minutes, or until the vegetables are tender.

3 Add the rice and soy sauce to the wok or pan and heat through thoroughly. Mix in the sesame seeds, if using.

4 Meanwhile, melt the butter in a small heavy-based frying pan and add the egg. Swirl the egg until it covers the base of the pan. Cook until the egg has set and is cooked through, then turn out onto a plate. Cut the omelette into strips or pieces.

5 Place the rice in a bowl and arrange the omelette on top.

sesame noodle stir-fry

Serves 2

  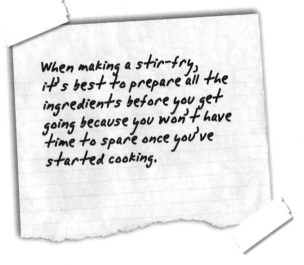

Ingredients

1 tsp red wine vinegar

1 tbsp soy sauce

1 tbsp tomato ketchup

2 tbsp orange juice

1 tsp clear honey

1 tsp cornflour

1 tbsp vegetable oil

100 g/3½ oz skinless, boneless chicken breast, cut into strips

2 spring onions, finely sliced

55 g/2 oz baby corn, halved lengthways

1 carrot, peeled and cut into thin batons

½ red pepper, deseeded and chopped

½ courgette, chopped

50 g/1¾ oz dried fine noodles

2 tsp sesame seeds

When making a stir-fry, it's best to prepare all the ingredients before you get going because you won't have time to spare once you've started cooking.

Method

1 Mix the vinegar, soy sauce, tomato ketchup, orange juice and honey together in a jug, add the cornflour and stir until well combined.

2 Heat the oil in a non-stick frying pan and stir-fry the chicken strips for 3–4 minutes. Add the vegetables and stir-fry for 4–5 minutes.

3 Add the cornflour mixture and bring to the boil, stirring constantly, then reduce the heat and simmer for 1 minute, until thickened.

4 Meanwhile, cook the noodles according to the packet instructions, drain and add to the pan along with the sesame seeds. Mix well. Serve hot or cold.

spaghetti olio e aglio

Serves 4

Ingredients

450 g/1 lb dried spaghetti

125 ml/4 fl oz extra virgin olive oil

3 garlic cloves, finely chopped

3 tbsp chopped fresh flat-leaf parsley

salt and pepper

Method

1 Bring a large saucepan of lightly salted water to the boil. Add the pasta, return to the boil and cook for 8–10 minutes, or until tender but still firm to the bite.

2 Meanwhile, heat the oil in a frying pan. Add the garlic and a pinch of salt and cook over a low heat, stirring constantly, for 3–4 minutes, or until golden. Do not allow the garlic to brown or it will taste bitter. Remove the frying pan from the heat.

3 Drain the pasta and transfer to a serving dish. Pour in the garlic-flavoured olive oil, then add the chopped parsley and season to taste with salt and pepper. Toss well and serve immediately.

spaghetti with tomatoes & basil

Serves 4

Ingredients

5 tbsp extra virgin olive oil

1 onion, finely chopped

800 g/1 lb 12 oz canned chopped tomatoes

4 garlic cloves, cut into quarters

450 g/1 lb dried spaghetti

large handful fresh basil leaves, shredded

salt and pepper

Parmesan cheese shavings, to serve

Method

1 Heat the oil in a large saucepan over a medium heat. Add the onion and cook gently for 5 minutes, until soft. Add the tomatoes and garlic. Bring to the boil, then simmer over a low–medium heat for 25–30 minutes, or until the oil separates from the tomatoes. Season to taste with salt and pepper.

2 Bring a large saucepan of lightly salted water to the boil. Add the pasta, return to the boil and cook for 8–10 minutes, or until tender but still firm to the bite. Drain and transfer to a serving dish.

3 Pour the sauce over the pasta. Add the basil and toss well to mix. Serve with the Parmesan cheese.

mushroom & spinach pasta

Serves 4

Ingredients

300 g/10½ oz dried penne

2 tbsp olive oil

250 g/9 oz mushrooms, sliced

1 tsp dried oregano

250 ml/9 fl oz vegetable stock

1 tbsp lemon juice

6 tbsp cream cheese

200 g/7 oz frozen spinach leaves

salt and pepper

Method

1 Bring a large saucepan of lightly salted water to the boil. Add the pasta, return to the boil and cook for 8–10 minutes, until tender but still firm to the bite. Drain, reserving 175 ml/6 fl oz of the cooking liquid.

2 Meanwhile, heat the oil in a large frying pan, add the mushrooms and cook, stirring frequently, for 8 minutes. Stir in the oregano, stock and lemon juice and cook for 10–12 minutes, or until reduced.

3 Stir in the cream cheese and spinach and cook over a low–medium heat for 3–5 minutes. Add the reserved cooking liquid, then the cooked pasta. Stir well, season to taste with salt and pepper and heat through before serving.

spaghetti alla carbonara

Serves 4

Ingredients

450 g/1 lb dried spaghetti

1 tbsp olive oil

225 g/8 oz streaky bacon, chopped

4 eggs

5 tbsp single cream

2 tbsp freshly grated Parmesan cheese

salt and pepper

Method

1 Bring a large saucepan of lightly salted water to the boil. Add the pasta, return to the boil and cook for 8–10 minutes, or until tender but still firm to the bite.

2 Meanwhile, heat the oil in a frying pan. Add the bacon and cook over a medium heat, stirring frequently, for 8–10 minutes.

3 Beat the eggs with the cream in a small bowl and season to taste with salt and pepper. Drain the pasta and return it to the saucepan. Tip in the contents of the frying pan, then add the egg mixture and half the Parmesan cheese. Stir well, then transfer to a serving dish. Serve immediately, sprinkled with the remaining cheese.

tuna-noodle casserole

Serves 4–6

Ingredients
200 g/7 oz dried tagliatelle

25 g/1 oz butter

55 g/2 oz fresh breadcrumbs

400 ml/14 fl oz canned condensed cream
  of mushroom soup

125 ml/4 fl oz milk

2 celery sticks, chopped

1 red and 1 green pepper, deseeded and
  chopped

140 g/5 oz mature Cheddar cheese,
  roughly grated

2 tbsp chopped fresh parsley

200 g/7 oz canned tuna in oil,
  drained and flaked

salt and pepper

> This recipe can easily be adapted to suit your tastes. For example, vegetarians can omit the tuna and add a couple of handfuls of chopped mushrooms.

Method

1 Preheat the oven to 200°C/400°F/Gas Mark 6. Bring a large saucepan of lightly salted water to the boil. Add the pasta and cook for 2 minutes fewer than specified on the packet instructions.

2 Meanwhile, melt the butter in a separate small saucepan over a medium heat. Stir in the breadcrumbs, then remove from the heat and reserve.

3 Drain the pasta well and reserve. Pour the soup into the pasta pan over a medium heat, then stir in the milk, celery, peppers, half the cheese and all the parsley. Add the tuna and gently stir in so that the flakes don't break up. Season to taste with salt and pepper. Heat just until small bubbles appear around the edge of the mixture – do not boil.

4 Stir the pasta into the pan and use 2 forks to mix all the ingredients together. Spoon the mixture into an ovenproof dish and spread out.

5 Stir the remaining cheese into the buttered breadcrumbs, then sprinkle over the top of the pasta mixture. Bake in the preheated oven for 20–25 minutes, until golden. Leave to stand for 5 minutes before serving straight from the dish.

macaroni cheese

Serves 4

Ingredients

600 ml/1 pint milk

1 onion, peeled

8 peppercorns

1 bay leaf

55 g/2 oz butter

40 g/1½ oz plain flour

½ tsp ground nutmeg

5 tbsp double cream

100 g/3½ oz mature Cheddar cheese, grated

100 g/3½ oz Roquefort cheese, crumbled

350 g/12 oz dried macaroni

100 g/3½ oz Gruyère or Emmental cheese, grated

pepper

> This is comfort food at its best! For a cheaper version of this dish, use just one type of cheese – a mature Cheddar would be a good choice.

STUDENT TASTE TEAM

Name: Lindsey Frost
Studying: Economics
At: Columbia University, USA
Comments about dish: This was a really lovely dish that I will certainly make again soon

Marks:
8/10

Method

1 Put the milk, onion, peppercorns and bay leaf in a pan and bring to the boil. Remove from the heat and leave to stand for 15 minutes.

2 Melt the butter in a pan and stir in the flour until well combined and smooth. Cook over a medium heat, stirring constantly, for 1 minute. Remove from the heat. Strain the milk to remove the solids and stir a little into the butter and flour mixture until well incorporated. Return to the heat and gradually add the remaining milk, stirring constantly, until it has all been incorporated. Cook for a further 3 minutes, or until the sauce is smooth and thickened, then add the nutmeg, cream and pepper to taste. Add the Cheddar and Roquefort cheeses and stir until melted.

3 Meanwhile, bring a large saucepan of water to the boil. Add the macaroni, return to the boil and cook for 8–10 minutes, or until tender but still firm to the bite. Drain well and add to the cheese sauce. Stir together well.

4 Preheat the grill to high. Spoon the mixture into an ovenproof dish, then scatter over the Gruyère cheese and cook under the grill until bubbling and brown.

meatloaf

Serves 6

Ingredients

450 g/1 lb lean beef mince

250 g/9 oz turkey or chicken mince

250 g/9 oz pork sausagemeat

2 slices wholemeal bread, made into crumbs

2 eggs, beaten

2 tsp dried Italian herbs

3 tbsp chopped fresh flat-leaf parsley

12 slices streaky bacon

500 g/1 lb 2 oz bottled passata with added onion

Method

1 Preheat the oven to 180°C/350°F/Gas Mark 4. Put the beef and turkey mince, sausagemeat, breadcrumbs, eggs, dried herbs and fresh parsley into a bowl and mix well, using your hands.

2 Line a 1-kg/2 lb 4-oz loaf tin with clingfilm. Put the meat mixture into the tin and press down very well. Invert the tin into a small roasting tin and remove the loaf tin and the clingfilm. Arrange the bacon rashers on top of the meatloaf, cover with foil and cook in the preheated oven for 1 hour.

3 Heat the passata in a small saucepan. Drain off any excess fat from around the meatloaf. Pour the passata into the roasting tin, brushing a little of the sauce over the meatloaf. Return to the oven for 5 minutes. Serve slices of the meatloaf with tomato sauce.

glazed gammon steaks

Serves 4

Ingredients

4 gammon steaks

4 tbsp dark brown sugar

2 tsp mustard powder

4 tbsp butter

8 slices canned pineapple, drained

Method

1 Preheat a griddle pan over a medium heat. Place the gammon steaks on it and cook for 5 minutes, turning once. If you have room for only 2 steaks at a time, cook them completely and keep warm while cooking the second pair.

2 Combine the brown sugar and mustard in a small bowl.

3 Melt the butter in a large frying pan. Add the pineapple and cook for 2 minutes to heat through, turning once. Sprinkle with the sugar and mustard mixture and continue cooking over a low heat until the sugar has melted and the pineapple is well glazed. Turn the pineapple once more so that both sides are coated with sauce.

4 Place the gammon steaks on individual plates and arrange 2 pineapple slices either next to them or overlapping on top. Spoon over some of the pan juices and serve.

Meat doesn't have to be off the menu when you're cooking on a budget – cheap cuts can be very tasty if cooked correctly.

94

sausages & mash with onion gravy

Serves 4

Ingredients
8 pork sausages

1 tbsp oil

Onion gravy
3 onions, cut in half and thinly sliced

70 g/2½ oz butter

250 ml/9 fl oz vegetable stock

salt and pepper

Mashed potato
900 g/2 lb floury potatoes, such as King
   Edwards, Maris Piper or Desirée, peeled
   and cut into chunks

55 g/2 oz butter

3 tbsp hot milk

2 tbsp chopped fresh parsley (optional)

salt and pepper

It pays to buy the best quality sausages you can afford – for a change, try ones with different seasonings. Vegetarians can use veggie sausages in place of the pork sausages.

Method

1 Cook the sausages slowly in a frying pan with the oil over a low heat. Cover the pan and turn the sausages from time to time. Don't rush the cooking because you want them well-cooked and sticky. This will take 25–30 minutes.

2 Meanwhile, prepare the onion gravy by placing the onions in a frying pan with the butter and frying over a low heat until soft, stirring continuously. Continue to cook until they are brown and almost melting, stirring from time to time. This will take about 30 minutes, but it is worth it as the onions will naturally caramelize.

3 Pour in the stock and continue to bubble away until the onion gravy is really thick. Season to taste with salt and pepper.

4 To make the mashed potato, cook the potatoes in a large saucepan of boiling salted water for 15–20 minutes. Drain well and mash with a potato masher until smooth. Season to taste with salt and pepper, add the butter, milk and parsley, if using, and stir well.

5 Serve the sausages with the mashed potato and the onion gravy spooned over the top.

boston baked beans

Serves 2

Ingredients

4 chipolata sausages

400 g/14 oz canned white beans such as haricot, cannellini or butter, drained and rinsed

200 ml/7 fl oz passata

1 tbsp maple syrup

1 tsp wholegrain mustard

4 rashers streaky bacon

This hearty American dish is a beefed-up version of baked beans. Serve on toast or as a topping for a jacket potato.

Method

1 Preheat the grill to high. Cook the sausages under the preheated grill, turning frequently, for about 10 minutes, or until browned and cooked through.

2 Put the beans, passata, maple syrup and mustard into a saucepan. Cook gently for about 10 minutes, until heated through.

3 Grill the bacon until crisp and browned. Either slice the sausages and add to the beans in the saucepan or serve the beans, topped with the bacon, alongside the sausages.

spicy fried eggs

Serves 2

Ingredients

2 tbsp olive oil

1 large onion, finely chopped

2 green or red peppers, deseeded and roughly chopped

1 garlic clove, finely chopped

½ tsp dried chilli flakes

4 plum tomatoes, peeled and roughly chopped

2 eggs

1 tbsp chopped fresh flat-leaf parsley (optional)

salt and pepper

Method

1 Heat the oil in a large non-stick frying pan over a medium heat. Add the onion and cook until golden. Add the peppers, garlic and chilli flakes and cook until the peppers are soft.

2 Stir in the tomatoes, season to taste with salt and pepper and simmer over a low–medium heat for 10 minutes.

3 Using the back of a spoon, make 2 depressions in the mixture in the frying pan. Break the eggs into the depressions, cover and cook for 3–4 minutes, until the eggs are set. Sprinkle with the parsley, if using, and serve.

pepper & mushroom hash

Serves 4

Ingredients

675 g/1 lb 8 oz potatoes, peeled and diced

1 tbsp olive oil

2 garlic cloves, crushed

1 green pepper, deseeded and diced

1 yellow pepper, deseeded and diced

3 tomatoes, diced

75 g/2¾ oz button mushrooms, halved

1 tbsp Worcestershire sauce

2 tbsp chopped fresh basil

salt and pepper

Method

1 Cook the potatoes in a large saucepan of lightly salted boiling water for 7–8 minutes. Drain well and reserve.

2 Heat the oil in a large frying pan. Add the potatoes and cook over a medium heat, stirring constantly, for about 8–10 minutes, until browned.

3 Add the garlic and peppers and cook, stirring frequently, for 2–3 minutes.

4 Stir in the tomatoes and mushrooms and cook, stirring frequently, for 5–6 minutes.

5 Stir in the Worcestershire sauce and basil and season to taste with salt and pepper. Transfer to a serving dish and serve.

These recipes are packed with vegetables, making them super-healthy but still really tasty!

potato skins with tomato & sweetcorn salsa

Serves 2

Ingredients

2 large baking potatoes

oil, for brushing

55 g/2 oz Cheddar cheese, grated

Salsa

85 g/3 oz canned sweetcorn kernels

55 g/2 oz canned kidney beans

2 tbsp olive oil

115 g/4 oz tomatoes, deseeded and diced

2 shallots, finely sliced

¼ red pepper, finely diced

1 fresh red chilli, deseeded and finely
  chopped

1 tbsp chopped fresh coriander leaves

1 tbsp lime juice

salt and pepper

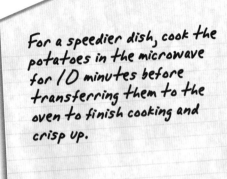

For a speedier dish, cook the potatoes in the microwave for 10 minutes before transferring them to the oven to finish cooking and crisp up.

Method

1 Preheat the oven to 200°C/400°F/Gas Mark 6. Prick the potatoes in several places with a fork and brush with oil. Cook directly on the oven shelf for 1 hour, or until the skins are crispy and the insides are soft when pierced with a fork.

2 Meanwhile, make the salsa. Drain the sweetcorn and beans, rinse well, then drain again. Put in a bowl with the oil, tomatoes, shallots, red pepper, chilli, coriander, lime juice and salt and pepper to taste and mix well together.

3 Preheat the grill to medium. Cut the potatoes in half lengthways. Scoop out the flesh (reserve for use in another recipe), leaving the skins intact. Brush the insides with oil, then put on a baking tray, cut-sides up. Cook under the grill for 5 minutes, or until crisp.

4 Spoon the salsa into the potato skins and sprinkle the cheese over the top. Return the filled potato skins to the grill and cook gently until the cheese has melted. Serve immediately.

beyond the takeout

Sometimes it can be difficult to resist the lure of the takeout, especially if you've had a drink or two. But if you do indulge, you'll soon find that takeout food isn't kind to the wallet, or to the waistline! The recipes in this chapter show how easy it is to make delicious takeout-style food at home at a fraction of the cost and, in many cases, calories. They are perfect for chilled-out nights in or lazy TV dinners.

thai green chicken curry

Serves 4

Ingredients

2 tbsp groundnut or sunflower oil

2 tbsp Thai green curry paste

500 g/1 lb 2 oz skinless, boneless chicken breasts, cut into chunks

2 kaffir lime leaves, roughly torn

1 lemon grass stalk, finely chopped

225 ml/8 fl oz coconut milk

2 aubergines, cut into chunks

2 tbsp Thai fish sauce

fresh Thai basil sprigs and thinly sliced kaffir lime leaves, to garnish

Most Thai ingredients are available in larger supermarkets. However, fresh kaffir lime leaves can be a little tricky to find - you can use dried ones, replace with lime zest or leave them out altogether.

Method

1 Heat the oil in a preheated wok or large, heavy-based frying pan. Add the curry paste and stir-fry briefly until all the aromas are released.

2 Add the chicken, lime leaves and lemon grass and stir-fry for 3–4 minutes, until the meat is beginning to colour.

3 Add the coconut milk and aubergines and simmer gently for 8–10 minutes, or until tender.

4 Stir in the fish sauce and serve immediately, garnished with sprigs of Thai basil and lime leaves.

vegetable korma

Serves 4

Ingredients

4 tbsp ghee or vegetable oil

2 onions, chopped

2 garlic cloves, chopped

1 fresh red chilli, chopped

1 tbsp grated fresh ginger

2 tomatoes, peeled and chopped

1 orange pepper, deseeded and cut into
   small pieces

1 large potato, peeled and cut into chunks

200 g/7 oz cauliflower florets

½ tsp salt

1 tsp ground turmeric

1 tsp ground cumin

1 tsp ground coriander

1 tsp garam masala

200 ml/7 fl oz vegetable stock or water

150 ml/5 fl oz natural yogurt

150 ml/5 fl oz single cream

25 g/1 oz fresh coriander, chopped

freshly cooked rice, to serve

When you add the yogurt and cream in step 5, be careful not to allow the mixture to come back to the boil – this would cause the yogurt and cream to curdle.

Method

1 Heat the ghee in a large saucepan over a medium heat, add the onions and garlic and cook, stirring, for 3 minutes.

2 Add the chilli and ginger and cook for a further 4 minutes.

3 Add the tomatoes, orange pepper, potato, cauliflower, salt and spices and cook, stirring, for a further 3 minutes.

4 Stir in the stock and bring to the boil. Reduce the heat and simmer for 25 minutes.

5 Stir in the yogurt and cream and cook gently, stirring, for a further 5 minutes. Add the fresh coriander and heat through. Serve with rice.

chicken chow mein

Serves 4

Ingredients

250 g/9 oz dried medium egg noodles

2 tbsp sunflower oil

275 g/9½ oz cooked chicken breasts, shredded

1 garlic clove, finely chopped

1 red pepper, deseeded and thinly sliced

100 g/3½ oz chestnut mushrooms, sliced

6 spring onions, sliced

100 g/3½ oz fresh beansprouts

3 tbsp soy sauce

1 tbsp sesame oil

Method

1. Cook the noodles according to the packet instructions.
2. Heat the sunflower oil in a large preheated wok. Add the chicken, garlic, red pepper, mushrooms, spring onions and beansprouts to the wok and stir-fry for about 5 minutes.
3. Drain the noodles thoroughly. Add the noodles to the wok, toss well and stir-fry for a further 5 minutes.
4. Drizzle the soy sauce and sesame oil over the chow mein and toss until well combined.
5. Transfer to serving bowls and serve immediately.

sesame hot noodles

Serves 6

Ingredients

500 g/18 oz dried medium egg noodles

3 tbsp sunflower oil

2 tbsp sesame oil

1 garlic clove, crushed

1 tbsp smooth peanut butter

1 small green chilli, deseeded and very finely chopped

3 tbsp toasted sesame seeds

4 tbsp light soy sauce

½ tbsp lime juice

4 tbsp chopped fresh coriander

salt and pepper

Method

1. Cook the noodles according to the packet instructions.
2. Meanwhile, make the dressing. Mix together the sunflower oil, sesame oil, garlic and peanut butter in a mixing bowl until smooth.
3. Add the chilli, sesame seeds and soy sauce to the bowl. Add the lime juice and mix well. Season to taste with salt and pepper.
4. Drain the noodles thoroughly, then place in a heated serving bowl.
5. Add the dressing and the chopped coriander to the noodles and toss well to mix. Serve hot.

If you don't have a wok, you can use a large frying pan or saucepan instead.

classic stir-fried vegetables

Serves 4

Ingredients

2 tbsp sesame oil

8 spring onions, finely chopped

1 garlic clove, crushed

1 tbsp grated fresh ginger

1 head of broccoli, cut into florets

1 orange or yellow pepper, roughly chopped

125 g/4½ oz red cabbage, shredded

125 g/4½ oz baby corn

175 g/6 oz portobello or large cup mushrooms, thinly sliced

200 g/7 oz fresh beansprouts

250 g/9 oz canned water chestnuts, drained

4 tsp soy sauce, or to taste

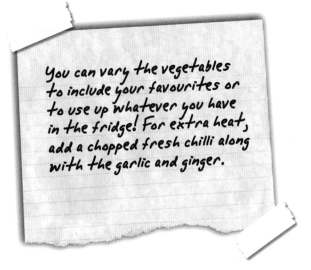

You can vary the vegetables to include your favourites or to use up whatever you have in the fridge! For extra heat, add a chopped fresh chilli along with the garlic and ginger.

Method

1 Heat the oil in a large wok over a high heat. Stir-fry three quarters of the spring onions with the garlic and ginger for 30 seconds.

2 Add the broccoli, pepper and red cabbage and stir-fry for 1–2 minutes. Mix in the baby corn and mushrooms and stir-fry for a further 1–2 minutes.

3 Finally, add the beansprouts and water chestnuts and cook for a further 2 minutes. Pour in the soy sauce to taste and stir well.

4 Transfer to serving dishes and serve immediately, garnished with the remaining spring onions.

chicken skewers with satay sauce

Serves 4

Ingredients

4 skinless chicken breasts, about 140 g/5 oz each

2 tbsp olive oil

2 tbsp lemon juice

Satay sauce

125 g/4½ oz smooth peanut butter

1½ tbsp olive oil

2 tbsp hot water

1½ tbsp light soy sauce

2 tbsp apple juice

4 tbsp coconut milk

Method

1 To make the satay sauce, mix all the ingredients together in a bowl.

2 Soak 16 wooden skewers in water for at least 30 minutes to prevent them from burning. Cut each chicken breast lengthways into 4 strips and thread each strip onto a skewer.

3 Mix the oil and lemon juice together in a small bowl, then brush over the chicken.

4 Preheat the grill to medium–high. Cook the chicken skewers for 3 minutes on each side, or until golden and cooked through, making sure that there is no trace of pink inside. Serve the skewers with the sauce.

Home-made kebabs are healthier than takeaway ones because you can control how much fat you add to them.

shish kebabs

Serves 4–6

Ingredients

500 g/1 lb 2 oz boneless leg or neck of lamb with a small amount of fat, cut into 2-cm/¾-inch cubes

2 green peppers, halved, deseeded and cut into 2-cm/¾-inch pieces

1 onion, quartered and separated into layers

2 cherry tomatoes per skewer

tzatziki and lemon wedges, to serve

Marinade

2 tbsp milk

2 tbsp olive oil, plus extra for brushing

1 large onion, grated

1 tbsp tomato purée

½ tsp ground cumin

salt and pepper

Method

1 To make the marinade, put all the ingredients in a bowl and stir until combined. Add the lamb cubes and mix to coat well with the marinade. Cover and leave to marinate in the refrigerator for 2 hours. If you are using wooden skewers, soak them in cold water for at least 30 minutes.

2 Preheat the grill to high. Lightly brush the pre-soaked wooden or metal skewers with oil, then thread an equal quantity of the lamb cubes onto each, alternating with pieces of green pepper and onion, and the cherry tomatoes.

3 Brush the grill rack with oil. Add the kebabs and cook, turning frequently and basting with the remaining marinade, for 8–10 minutes, or until the lamb and peppers are charred on the edges.

4 Serve the kebabs with tzatziki and lemon wedges.

vegetable chilli

Serves 4

Ingredients

1 aubergine, cut into 2.5-cm/1-inch slices

1 tbsp olive oil, plus extra for brushing

1 large red onion, finely chopped

2 red or yellow peppers, deseeded and
finely chopped

3–4 garlic cloves, finely chopped or
crushed

800 g/1 lb 12 oz canned chopped
tomatoes

1 tbsp mild chilli powder

½ tsp ground cumin

½ tsp dried oregano

2 small courgettes, quartered lengthways
and sliced

400 g/14 oz canned kidney beans, drained
and rinsed

450 ml/16 fl oz water

1 tbsp tomato purée

6 spring onions, finely chopped

115 g/4 oz Cheddar cheese, grated

salt and pepper

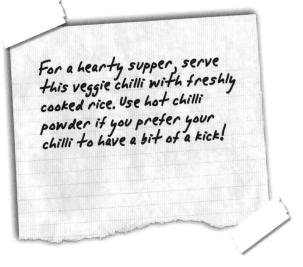

For a hearty supper, serve this veggie chilli with freshly cooked rice. Use hot chilli powder if you prefer your chilli to have a bit of a kick!

Method

1 Brush the aubergine slices on one side with oil. Heat half the oil in a large heavy-based frying pan over a medium–high heat. Add the aubergine slices, oiled-side up, and cook for 5–6 minutes, or until browned on one side. Turn over the slices, cook on the other side until browned and transfer to a plate. Cut into bite-sized pieces.

2 Heat the remaining oil in a large saucepan over a medium heat. Add the onion and peppers and cook, stirring occasionally, for 3–4 minutes, or until the onion is just softened but not browned.

3 Add the garlic and cook for a further 2–3 minutes, or until the onion is beginning to colour.

4 Add the tomatoes, chilli powder, cumin and oregano. Season to taste with salt and pepper. Bring to the boil, reduce the heat, cover and simmer for 15 minutes.

5 Add the courgettes, aubergine and kidney beans. Stir in the water and the tomato purée. Return to the boil, then cover and continue simmering for 45 minutes, or until the vegetables are tender. Ladle into bowls and top with the spring onions and cheese.

chilli con carne

Serves 4

Ingredients

2 tbsp sunflower oil

500 g/1 lb 2 oz fresh beef mince

1 large onion, chopped

1 garlic clove, finely chopped

1 green pepper, deseeded and diced

1 tsp chilli powder

800 g/1 lb 12 oz canned chopped tomatoes

800 g/1 lb 12 oz canned red kidney beans,
   drained and rinsed

450 ml/16 fl oz beef stock

handful of fresh coriander sprigs (optional)

salt and pepper

freshly cooked rice and soured cream, to serve

Method

1 Heat the oil in a large heavy-based saucepan or
   flameproof casserole. Add the mince and cook over
   a medium heat, stirring frequently, for 5 minutes, or
   until broken up and browned.

2 Reduce the heat, then add the onion, garlic
   and green pepper to the pan and cook, stirring
   frequently, for 10 minutes.

3 Stir in the chilli powder, tomatoes and kidney
   beans. Pour in the stock and season to taste with
   salt. Bring to the boil, reduce the heat and simmer,
   stirring frequently, for about 15–20 minutes, or
   until the meat is tender.

4 Chop the coriander sprigs, if using, and stir into the
   pan. Serve with rice and soured cream.

nachos

Serves 6

Ingredients

175 g/6 oz tortilla chips

400 g/14 oz canned refried beans, warmed

2 tbsp finely chopped bottled jalapeño chillies

200 g/7 oz canned or bottled pimentos or roasted
   peppers, drained and finely sliced

115 g/4 oz Gruyère cheese, grated

115 g/4 oz Cheddar cheese, grated

salt and pepper

Method

1 Preheat the oven to 200°C/400°F/Gas Mark 6.

2 Spread the tortilla chips out over the base of a
   large, shallow, ovenproof dish or roasting tin. Cover
   with the warmed refried beans. Scatter over the
   chillies and pimentos and season to taste with salt
   and pepper. Mix the cheeses together in a bowl and
   sprinkle on top.

3 Bake in the preheated oven for 5–8 minutes, or
   until the cheese is bubbling and melted. Serve
   immediately.

Any leftover chilli con carne will taste even better the next day as the delicious flavours will have had time to deepen.

chicken fajitas with guacamole

Serves 4

Ingredients
1 tsp ground cumin

1 tbsp olive oil, plus extra for brushing

1 garlic clove, sliced

juice of 1 lime

4 chicken breasts, about 115 g/4 oz each,
    cut into strips

4 flour tortillas

1 red pepper, deseeded and sliced

2 spring onions, diagonally sliced

salt and pepper

Guacamole
1 large avocado, halved and stoned

1 garlic clove, crushed

juice of ½ lime

1 tbsp mayonnaise

salt and pepper

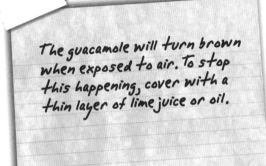

The guacamole will turn brown when exposed to air. To stop this happening, cover with a thin layer of lime juice or oil.

STUDENT TASTE TEAM

Name: Chemaine Shehadeh

Studying: Civil Engineering

At: University of Technology, Sydney, Australia

Comments about dish: This was very easy to make

Marks: 8/10

Method

1 Mix the cumin, oil, garlic and lime juice together in a non-metallic shallow dish. Season the chicken to taste with salt and pepper, add to the dish and turn to coat in the marinade. Cover with clingfilm and leave to marinate in the refrigerator for up to 1 hour, turning the chicken occasionally.

2 To make the guacamole, scoop the flesh from the avocado halves into a bowl and mash together with the garlic and lime juice. Add the mayonnaise and salt and pepper to taste and mix until smooth and creamy. Set aside.

3 Preheat a griddle pan. Remove the chicken from the marinade, brush with oil and cook for 6–8 minutes, turning halfway through the cooking time, until cooked through and golden.

4 Meanwhile, warm the tortillas according to the packet instructions. Arrange an equal quantity of the chicken, red pepper and spring onions down the centre of each. Add a spoonful of guacamole and roll up. Slice diagonally in half to serve.

beef burgers

Serves 4

Ingredients

750 g/1 lb 10 oz fresh beef mince

1 beef stock cube

1 tbsp minced dried onion

2 tbsp water

55 g/2 oz grated Cheddar cheese (optional)

4 burger buns, split

tomato ketchup, tomato slices and lettuce leaves, to serve

Method

1 Place the mince in a large mixing bowl. Crumble the stock cube over the meat, add the dried onion and water and mix well. Divide the meat into 4 portions, shape each into a ball, then flatten slightly to make a burger shape of your preferred thickness.

2 Preheat a griddle pan over a high heat. Cook the burgers for about 5 minutes on each side, depending on how well done you like your meat and the thickness of the burgers. Press down occasionally with a spatula or palette knife during cooking.

3 To make cheeseburgers, sprinkle the cheese on top of the burgers after you have turned them.

4 Serve the burgers in buns with tomato ketchup, tomato slices and lettuce leaves.

bean burgers

Serves 6

Ingredients

400 g/14 oz canned cannellini beans, drained and rinsed

2 tbsp red pesto

75 g/2¾ oz fresh wholemeal breadcrumbs

1 egg

2 tbsp olive oil

½ small red onion, finely chopped

1 garlic clove, crushed

6 Granary rolls

6 tsp hummus

salt and pepper

tomato slices, cucumber slices and lettuce leaves, to serve

Method

1 Mash the beans with a potato masher in a bowl until they are smooth, then add the pesto, breadcrumbs, egg and salt and pepper to taste, and mix well.

2 Heat half the oil in a non-stick frying pan over a low heat and cook the onion and garlic until soft. Add to the bean mixture and mix well.

3 Heat the remaining oil in the frying pan. Spoon in the bean mixture, in 6 separate mounds, then press each one down with the back of a spoon to form a burger.

4 Cook the burgers for 4–5 minutes, then carefully turn over and cook for a further 4–5 minutes, until golden.

5 Meanwhile, slice the rolls in half and spread the bottom half of each roll with a teaspoon of the hummus.

6 Remove the burgers from the frying pan and drain on kitchen paper. Place each one in a roll, and top with the tomato and cucumber slices and lettuce leaves.

122

Home-made burgers are simple and fun to make. If you have time, chill the burgers in the fridge before cooking – this will help them keep their shape.

pizza

Serves 2

Ingredients
Pizza base

225 g/8 oz strong white flour,
plus extra for dusting

1 tsp easy-blend dried yeast

1 tsp salt

2 tbsp olive oil

225–350 ml/8–12 fl oz warm water

Topping

4 tbsp olive oil

1 large onion, thinly sliced

6 button mushrooms, thinly sliced

½ small green pepper, ½ small red pepper
and ½ small yellow pepper, deseeded
and thinly sliced

300 g/10½ oz ready-made tomato
pasta sauce

55 g/2 oz mozzarella cheese, thickly sliced

2 tbsp freshly grated Parmesan cheese

1 tsp chopped fresh basil

> Kneading pizza dough is a great stress-buster! For the best results, you will need to knead the dough for at least 10 minutes. Alternatively, you could use ready-made pizza bases.

Method

1 Combine the flour, yeast and salt in a mixing bowl. Drizzle over half the oil. Make a well in the centre and pour in the water. Mix to a firm dough and shape into a ball. Turn out onto a floured work surface and knead until it is smooth and elastic. Brush the bowl with the remaining oil. Put the dough in the bowl and turn to coat with oil. Cover with a clean tea towel and leave to rise for 1 hour.

2 When the dough has doubled in size, punch it down to release the excess air, then knead until smooth. Divide in half and roll into 2 thin rounds. Place on a baking sheet.

3 Preheat the oven to 220°C/425°F/Gas Mark 7. For the topping, heat the oil in a frying-pan and cook the onion, mushrooms and peppers for 5 minutes, or until softened. Spread some of the tomato sauce over the pizza bases, but do not go right to the edge. Top with the vegetables and mozzarella cheese. Spoon over more tomato sauce, then sprinkle with Parmesan cheese and basil. Bake in the preheated oven for 10–15 minutes, or until the base is crispy and the cheese has melted.

home-made oven chips

Serves 4

Ingredients

450 g/1 lb potatoes, peeled

2 tbsp sunflower oil

salt and pepper

Method

1 Preheat the oven to 200°C/400°F/Gas Mark 6.

2 Cut the potatoes into thick, even-sized chips. Rinse them under cold running water and then dry well on a clean tea towel. Put in a bowl, add the oil and toss together until coated.

3 Spread the chips on a baking sheet and cook in the oven for 40–45 minutes, turning once, until golden. Add salt and pepper to taste and serve hot.

fish cakes

Serves 4

Ingredients

450 g/1 lb potatoes, peeled

450 g/1 lb mixed fish fillets, such as cod, haddock and salmon, skinned

2 tbsp chopped fresh parsley or tarragon

grated rind of 1 lemon

1 tbsp plain flour

1 egg, beaten

115 g/4 oz white or wholemeal breadcrumbs, made from day-old bread

4 tbsp vegetable oil

salt and pepper

Method

1 Cut the potatoes into chunks and cook in a large saucepan of salted boiling water for 15 minutes. Drain well and mash with a potato masher until smooth.

2 Place the fish in a frying pan and just cover with water. Bring to the boil over a medium heat, then cover and simmer gently for 5 minutes, until just cooked. Remove from the heat and drain the fish onto a plate. When cool enough to handle, flake the fish and ensure that no bones remain.

3 Mix the potatoes with the fish, parsley and lemon rind in a bowl. Season well with salt and pepper and shape into four round, flat cakes.

4 Dust the fish cakes with flour, dip them into the beaten egg, then coat thoroughly in the breadcrumbs. Place on a baking sheet, cover with clingfilm and chill in the refrigerator for at least 30 minutes.

5 Heat the oil in the frying pan and fry the fish cakes over a medium heat for 5 minutes on each side. Use a palette knife or fish slice to turn them carefully. Serve.

If funds are running low, use canned drained salmon for the fish cakes instead of fresh fish.

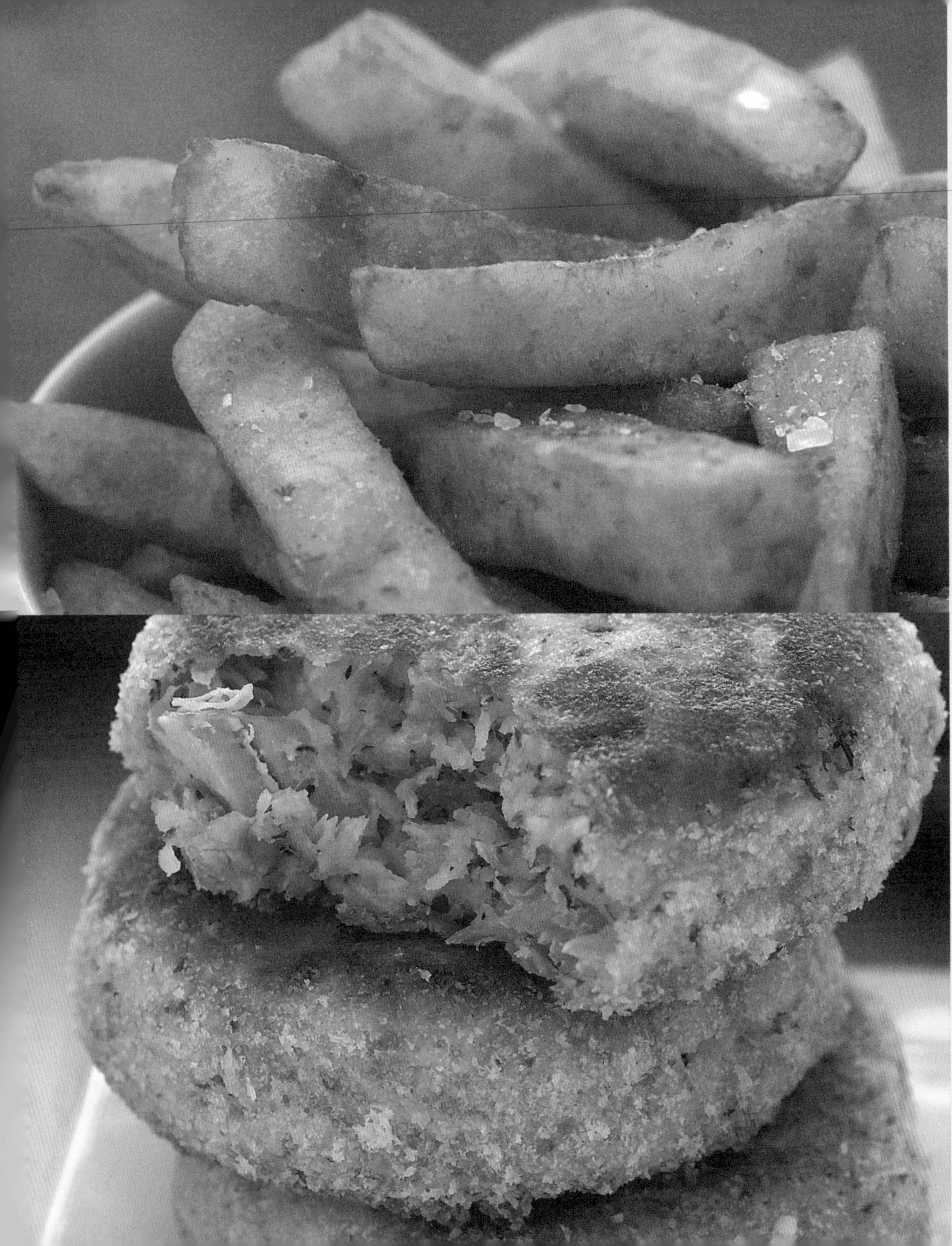

chicken nuggets

Serves 4

Ingredients

4 tbsp dry breadcrumbs

2 tbsp finely grated Parmesan cheese

1 tsp dried thyme

1 tsp salt

pinch of pepper

2 skinless, boneless chicken breasts, cut into cubes

115 g/4 oz melted butter

barbecue sauce or tomato ketchup, to serve

Method

1 Preheat the oven to 200°C/400°F/Gas Mark 6. Combine the breadcrumbs, cheese, thyme, salt and pepper on a large plate or in a polythene bag.

2 Toss the chicken cubes in the melted butter, then in the crumb mixture. Place on a baking sheet and bake in the preheated oven for 10 minutes, until crisp.

3 Remove the chicken nuggets from the oven and serve with barbecue sauce or tomato ketchup.

falafel

Serves 4

Ingredients

225 g/8 oz dried chickpeas

1 large onion, finely chopped

1 garlic clove, crushed

2 tbsp chopped fresh parsley

2 tsp ground cumin

2 tsp ground coriander

½ tsp baking powder

oil, for deep-frying

salt and cayenne pepper

hummus, tomato wedges and parsley sprigs, to serve

Method

1 Soak the chickpeas overnight in enough cold water to cover them and allow room for expansion. Drain, then place in a saucepan, cover with fresh water and bring to the boil. Reduce the heat and simmer for 1 hour, or until tender. Drain.

2 Place the chickpeas in a food processor and blend to make a coarse paste. Add the onion, garlic, parsley, cumin, coriander, baking powder, and salt and cayenne pepper to taste. Blend again to mix thoroughly. Alternatively, mash the chickpeas in a bowl with a potato masher, then stir in the remaining ingredients.

3 Cover and leave to rest for 30 minutes, then shape into balls. Leave to rest for a further 30 minutes. Heat the oil in a deep-fat fryer or large saucepan to 180–190°C/350–375°F, or until a cube of bread browns in 30 seconds. Carefully drop in the balls and cook until golden brown. Remove from the oil and drain on kitchen paper.

4 Serve hot or at room temperature with hummus, tomato wedges and parsley sprigs.

For falafel in a flash, use canned chickpeas in place of the dried chickpeas.

hummus

Serves 6

Ingredients

400 g/14 oz canned chickpeas, drained

150 ml/5 fl oz tahini, well stirred

150 ml/5 fl oz olive oil, plus extra for drizzling

2 garlic cloves, roughly chopped

6 tbsp lemon juice

1 tbsp chopped fresh mint

salt and pepper

paprika, to serve

Method

1 Put the chickpeas, tahini, oil and 150 ml/5 fl oz water into a tall beaker and process briefly using a hand-held stick blender. Add the garlic, lemon juice and mint and process until smooth.

2 Check the consistency of the hummus and, if it is too thick, add 1 tablespoon of water and process again. Continue adding water, 1 tablespoon at a time, until the right consistency is achieved. Hummus should have a thick, coating consistency. Season to taste with salt and pepper.

3 Spoon the hummus into a serving dish and drizzle with a little oil. Cover with clingfilm and chill until required. To serve, dust lightly with paprika.

pitta crisps

Makes 16

Ingredients

2 wholemeal pitta breads

olive oil, for brushing

Method

1 Preheat the oven to 180ºC/350ºF/Gas Mark 4. Using a serrated knife, split each pitta bread in half, then quarter each half to make a total of 16 pieces.

2 Place the pieces of pitta bread on a baking sheet, rough side up. Lightly brush each piece with oil, then bake in the preheated oven for 20 minutes, or until crisp and golden brown.

3 Leave to cool completely before serving with dips. These crisps will keep fresh in an airtight container for up to 3 days.

paprika crisps

Serves 4

Ingredients

2 large potatoes, peeled

3 tbsp olive oil

½ tsp paprika

salt

Method

1 Slice the potatoes very thinly so that they are almost transparent and place in a bowl of cold water, then drain them thoroughly and pat dry with kitchen paper.

2 Heat the oil in a large heavy-based frying pan and add the paprika. Cook, stirring constantly to ensure that the paprika doesn't catch on the base and burn.

3 Add the potato slices to the frying pan and cook them in a single layer over a low–medium heat for about 5 minutes, or until the potato slices are just beginning to curl slightly at the edges.

4 Remove the potato slices from the pan using a slotted spoon and transfer them to kitchen paper to drain thoroughly.

5 Preheat the grill to medium. Sprinkle the potato slices with salt and cook under the preheated grill, turning frequently, for 10 minutes, until they begin to go crisp. Sprinkle with a little more salt and serve immediately.

chocolate popcorn

Serves 2

Ingredients

3 tbsp sunflower oil

70 g/2½ oz popping corn

25 g/1 oz butter

55 g/2 oz soft light brown sugar

2 tbsp golden syrup

1 tbsp milk

55 g/2 oz plain chocolate chips

Method

1 Preheat the oven to 150°C/300°F/Gas Mark 2. Heat the oil in a large heavy-based saucepan. Add the popping corn, cover and cook, shaking the saucepan vigorously, for about 2 minutes, until the popping stops. Turn into a large bowl.

2 Put the butter, sugar, golden syrup and milk in a saucepan and heat gently until the butter has melted. Bring to the boil, without stirring, and boil for 2 minutes. Remove from the heat, add the chocolate chips and stir until melted.

3 Pour the chocolate mixture over the popcorn and toss together until evenly coated. Spread the mixture onto a large baking tray.

4 Bake the popcorn in the preheated oven for about 15 minutes, until crisp.

iced raspberry sundae

Serves 4

Ingredients

450 g/1 lb fresh raspberries,
   plus extra to decorate

450 ml/16 fl oz double cream

55 g/2 oz flaked almonds

225 g/8 oz fresh or canned cherries,
   stoned

15 g/½ oz plain chocolate, grated

fresh mint sprigs, to decorate

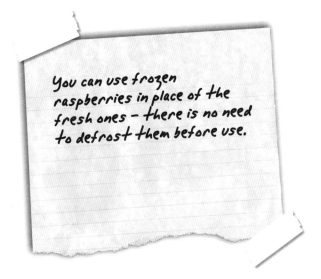

You can use frozen raspberries in place of the fresh ones – there is no need to defrost them before use.

Method

1 Preheat the oven to 200°C/400°F/Gas Mark 6. Reserve 115 g/4 oz of the raspberries and lightly crush the remainder.

2 Whip the cream in a medium bowl until soft peaks form. Put 4 tablespoons of the cream into a small bowl, cover and reserve. Stir the crushed raspberries into the remaining cream, spoon into a freezerproof container and freeze for 1 hour, or until partially frozen.

3 Meanwhile, spread the almonds out on a baking sheet and toast in the preheated oven, turning occasionally, for 8–10 minutes, or until golden brown. Remove from the oven and leave to cool.

4 Arrange the reserved raspberries and cherries in the bases of 4 sundae glasses, then sprinkle with a few toasted almonds. Cover with scoops of the frozen raspberry mixture, then swirl the reserved cream on top. Sprinkle with the grated chocolate and decorate with extra raspberries and mint sprigs.

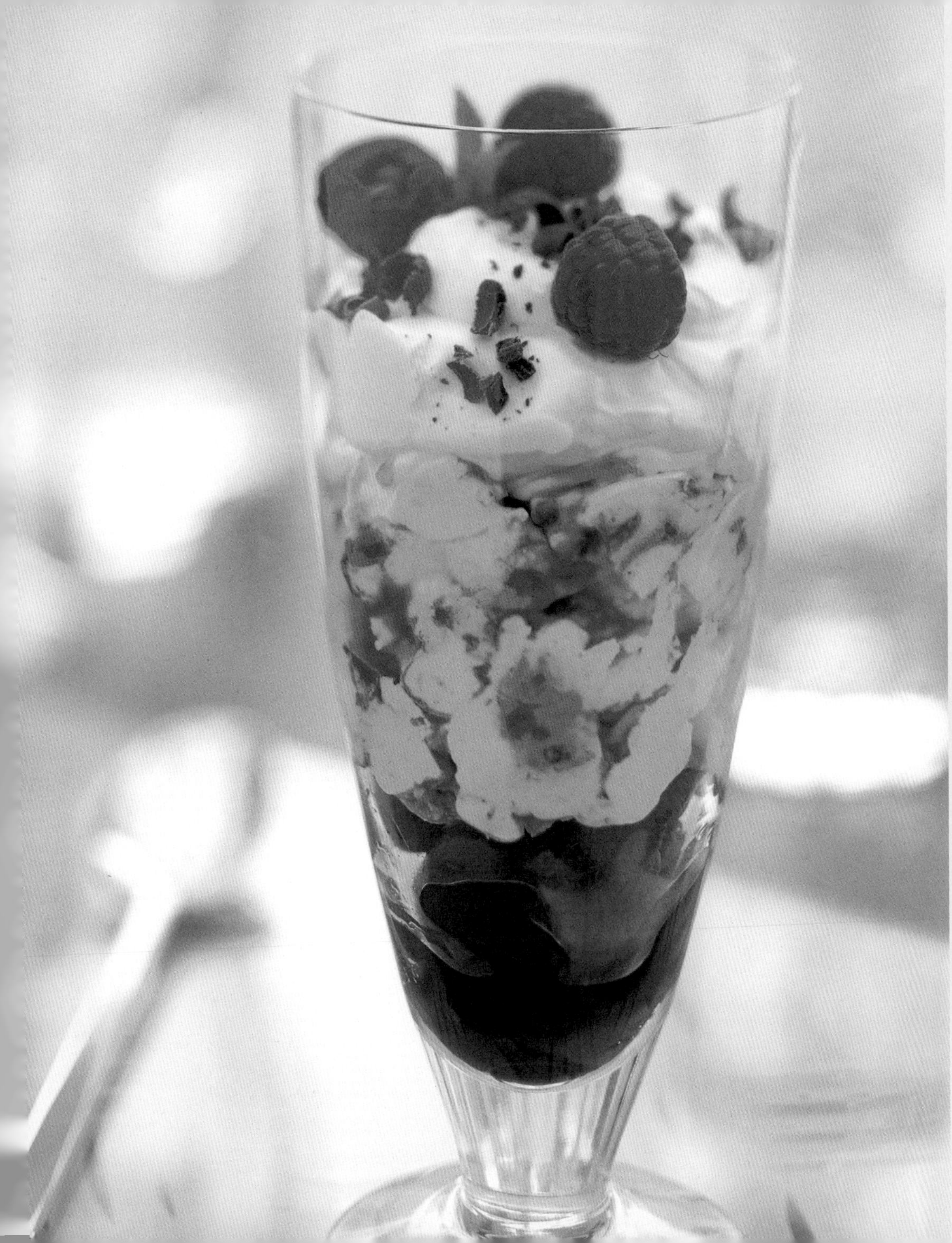

chocolate ice-cream bites

Serves 6

Ingredients

600 ml/1 pint ice cream
200 g/7 oz plain chocolate, broken into pieces
2 tbsp unsalted butter

Method

1 Line a baking tray with clingfilm.

2 Using a melon baller, scoop out balls of ice cream and place them on the prepared baking tray. Alternatively, cut the ice cream into bite-sized cubes. Stick a cocktail stick in each piece and return to the freezer until very hard.

3 Place the chocolate and the butter in a heatproof bowl set over a saucepan of gently simmering water until melted. Quickly dip the frozen ice-cream balls into the warm chocolate and return to the freezer. Keep them there until ready to serve.

fruit skewers

Serves 2

Ingredients

a selection of fruit, such as apricots, peaches, figs, strawberries, mangoes, pineapple, bananas, dates and pawpaw, prepared and cut into chunks
2 tbsp maple syrup
50 g/1¾ oz plain chocolate, broken into pieces

Method

1 Soak 4 wooden skewers in water for at least 30 minutes.

2 Preheat the grill to high and line the grill pan with foil. Thread alternate pieces of fruit onto each skewer. Brush the fruit with a little maple syrup.

3 Put the chocolate in a heatproof bowl set over a saucepan of gently simmering water, ensuring that the bowl does not touch the water, and heat until the chocolate has melted.

4 Meanwhile, cook the fruit skewers under the preheated grill for 3 minutes, or until caramelized. Serve drizzled with the melted chocolate.

Plain chocolate is a very useful ingredient to have in your store cupboard – if you can resist temptation, that is!

look who's cooking

Once you've been cooking for a while and feel you've mastered the basics, you'll be ready to take on a new challenge – cooking to impress. Whether you want to cook a romantic dinner for a hot date or a slap-up meal for your parents, this chapter is packed with ideas for restaurant-style dishes that are sure to fit the bill. Even better, they won't break the bank so you don't need to limit them to special occasions.

spag bol

Serves 4

Ingredients

2 tbsp olive oil

1 onion, finely chopped

2 garlic cloves, finely chopped

1 carrot, peeled and finely chopped

85 g/3 oz mushrooms, sliced

1 tsp dried oregano

½ tsp dried thyme

1 bay leaf

280 g/10 oz fresh beef mince

300 ml/10 fl oz beef stock

300 ml/10 fl oz passata

350 g/12 oz dried spaghetti

salt and pepper

Method

1 To make the sauce, heat the oil in a heavy-based, non-stick saucepan. Add the onion and sauté, half covered, for 5 minutes, or until softened. Add the garlic, carrot and mushrooms and sauté for a further 3 minutes, stirring occasionally.

2 Add the herbs and mince to the pan and cook until the meat has browned, stirring regularly.

3 Add the stock and passata. Reduce the heat, season to taste with salt and pepper and cook over a low–medium heat, half covered, for 15–20 minutes, or until the sauce has reduced and thickened. Remove the bay leaf.

4 Meanwhile, bring a large saucepan of lightly salted water to the boil. Add the pasta, return to the boil and cook for 8–10 minutes, until tender but still firm to the bite.

5 Drain the pasta, then mix together the pasta and sauce. Serve immediately.

spaghetti with meatballs

Serves 4

Ingredients

40 g/1½ oz fresh breadcrumbs

400 g/14 oz fresh beef mince

2 garlic cloves, crushed

1 large egg, lightly beaten

40 g/1½ oz Parmesan cheese, finely grated

flour, for coating

2 tbsp olive oil

2 garlic cloves, crushed

2 tsp dried oregano

800 g/1 lb 12 oz canned chopped tomatoes

1 tbsp tomato purée

1 tsp sugar

300 g/10½ oz dried spaghetti

salt and pepper

Method

1 Place the breadcrumbs in a bowl with the beef, garlic, egg, cheese and salt and pepper to taste.

2 Mix the beef mixture until it comes together in a ball. Flour your hands and roll the mixture into walnut-sized balls.

3 Chill the meatballs in the refrigerator while you make the sauce. Heat the oil in a saucepan and add the garlic and oregano. Stir for 1 minute.

4 Add the tomatoes, tomato purée and sugar. Bring to the boil, then reduce the heat and simmer for 8 minutes.

5 Carefully place the meatballs in the pan and spoon the sauce over them. Cover and simmer for 20 minutes, turning the meatballs occasionally.

6 Meanwhile, bring a large saucepan of lightly salted water to the boil. Add the pasta, return to the boil and cook for 8–10 minutes, until tender but still firm to the bite. Drain and serve with the meatballs and sauce.

beef bourguignon

Serves 6

Ingredients

2 tbsp olive oil

175 g/6 oz unsmoked bacon,
  sliced into thin strips

1.3 kg/3 lb braising beef, cut into
  5-cm/2-inch pieces

2 carrots, peeled and sliced

2 onions, chopped

2 garlic cloves, very finely chopped

3 tbsp plain flour

700 ml/1¼ pints red wine

350–450 ml/12–16 fl oz beef stock

1 sachet bouquet garni

1 tsp salt

¼ tsp pepper

3 tbsp butter

350 g/12 oz shallots

350 g/12 oz button mushrooms

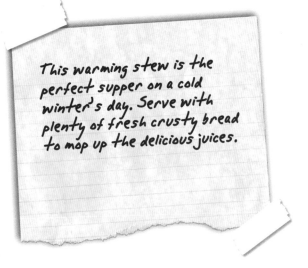

This warming stew is the perfect supper on a cold winter's day. Serve with plenty of fresh crusty bread to mop up the delicious juices.

Method

1 Heat the oil in a large flameproof casserole over a medium heat. Add the bacon and brown for 2–3 minutes. Remove with a slotted spoon. Add the beef in batches and cook until browned. Drain and set aside with the bacon. Add the carrots and chopped onions to the casserole and cook for 5 minutes. Add the garlic and fry until just coloured. Return the meat and bacon to the casserole. Sprinkle over the flour and cook for 1 minute, stirring. Add the wine, enough stock to cover, the bouquet garni, salt and pepper. Bring to the boil, cover and simmer gently for 3 hours.

2 Heat half the butter in a frying pan. Add the shallots, cover and cook until softened. Remove with a slotted spoon and keep warm. Heat the remaining butter in the frying pan. Add the mushrooms and fry briefly. Remove and keep warm.

3 Strain the casserole liquid through a sieve into a clean saucepan. Wipe out the casserole with kitchen paper and tip the meat mixture, mushrooms and shallots back in. Remove the surface fat from the cooking liquid, simmer for 1–2 minutes to reduce, then pour over the meat and vegetables. Serve.

beef goulash

Serves 4

Ingredients

2 tbsp vegetable oil

1 large onion, chopped

1 garlic clove, crushed

750 g/1 lb 10 oz lean braising beef

2 tbsp paprika

400 g/14 oz canned chopped tomatoes

2 tbsp tomato purée

1 large red pepper, deseeded and chopped

175 g/6 oz button mushrooms, sliced

600 ml/1 pint beef stock

1 tbsp cornflour

1 tbsp water

salt and pepper

chopped fresh parsley, to garnish

freshly cooked long-grain and wild rice,
    to serve

> Cooking meat in this way makes it so tender that it practically melts in your mouth. Braising beef is very economical and is an ideal choice for anyone who's watching their pennies!

Method

1 Heat the vegetable oil in a large heavy-based frying pan. Add the onion and garlic and cook over a low heat for 3–4 minutes.

2 Using a sharp knife, cut the beef into chunks, add to the frying pan and cook over a high heat for 3 minutes, or until browned. Add the paprika and stir well, then add the tomatoes, tomato purée, red pepper and mushrooms. Cook for a further 2 minutes, stirring frequently. Pour in the stock. Bring to the boil, reduce the heat, cover and simmer for 1½–2 hours, or until the meat is tender.

3 Blend the cornflour and water together in a small bowl, then add to the frying pan, stirring, until thickened and smooth. Cook for 1 minute. Season to taste with salt and pepper.

4 Transfer the beef goulash to a serving dish, garnish with parsley and serve with a mix of long-grain and wild rice.

roast chicken

Serves 6

Ingredients

1 chicken, weighing 2.25 kg/5 lb

55 g/2 oz butter

2 tbsp chopped fresh lemon thyme

1 lemon, quartered

125 ml/4 fl oz white wine

salt and pepper

roast potatoes, to serve

> To make gravy, spoon off the fat from the roasting tin, then place the tin over a low heat on the hob. Add a little stock or wine and simmer until reduced and thickened.

Method

1 Preheat the oven to 220°C/425°F/Gas Mark 7. Make sure the chicken is clean, wiping it inside and out using kitchen paper, and place in a roasting tin.

2 Place the butter in a bowl and mash with a fork, then mix in the thyme and season well with salt and pepper. Butter the chicken all over with the herb butter, inside and out, and place the lemon quarters inside the body cavity. Pour the wine over the chicken.

3 Roast the chicken in the centre of the preheated oven for 20 minutes. Reduce the temperature to 190°C/375°F/Gas Mark 5 and continue to roast for a further 1¼ hours, basting frequently. Cover with foil if the skin begins to brown too much. If the tin dries out, add a little more wine or water.

4 Test that the chicken is cooked by piercing the thickest part of the leg with a sharp knife or skewer and making sure the juices run clear. Remove from the oven.

5 Remove the chicken from the roasting tin and place on a warmed serving plate to rest, covered with foil, for 10 minutes before carving.

6 Serve with roast potatoes and gravy (see above).

southern fried chicken

Serves 4–6

Ingredients

1 chicken, weighing 1.5 kg/3 lb 5 oz,
   cut into 6–8 pieces

75 g/2¾ oz plain flour

2–4 tbsp butter

corn or groundnut oil, for shallow-frying

salt and pepper

Buying a whole chicken and jointing it yourself (or asking your butcher to do it) is usually cheaper than buying chicken portions. This dish could also be made using chicken drumsticks.

Method

1 Put the chicken into a large bowl with 1 teaspoon of salt and enough water to cover, then cover and chill in the refrigerator for at least 4 hours, but ideally overnight. Drain well and pat dry with kitchen paper.

2 Put the flour and salt and pepper to taste into a polythene bag. Add the chicken pieces and shake until well coated. Remove the chicken pieces from the bag and shake off any excess flour.

3 Melt 2 tablespoons of the butter with about 1 cm/ ½ inch of oil in a flameproof casserole or large frying pan with a lid over a medium–high heat. Do not leave unattended.

4 Add as many chicken pieces as will fit in a single layer without overcrowding, skin-side down. Cook for 5 minutes, or until the skin is golden and crisp. Turn the chicken over and cook for a further 10–15 minutes, covered, until the juices run clear when a skewer is inserted into the thickest part of the meat. Remove the chicken from the casserole and drain well on kitchen paper. Transfer to a low oven to keep warm while cooking any remaining pieces, adding more butter and oil if necessary.

paella

Serves 2–3

Ingredients

2 tbsp olive oil

1 onion, diced

2 skinless chicken breasts, sliced

1 small red pepper, deseeded and diced

2 garlic cloves, chopped

1 tomato, deseeded and chopped

1 tbsp tomato purée

½ tsp ground turmeric

600 ml/1 pint chicken stock or vegetable stock

175 g/6 oz paella rice

55 g/2 oz frozen peas

115 g/4 oz cooked prawns, thawed if frozen

salt and pepper

Do not stir the paella during cooking, but shake the pan once or twice. The paella is ready when you smell a faint toasty aroma coming from the rice. If you're feeling flush, use saffron instead of the turmeric for a more authentic flavour.

Method

1 Heat the oil in a large heavy-based frying pan with a lid. Add the onion and fry for 5 minutes, or until soft. Add the chicken, red pepper and garlic and sauté for 5 minutes over a medium heat, stirring frequently to prevent the mixture from sticking to the base of the pan.

2 Add the tomato, tomato purée, turmeric and stock to the pan. Stir in the rice and bring to the boil, then reduce the heat and simmer, covered, for 15 minutes, or until the rice is tender.

3 Add the peas, prawns and salt and pepper to taste and cook for a further 2–3 minutes, or until the prawns have heated through.

roast vegetable lasagne

Serves 4

Ingredients

3 tbsp olive oil

4 courgettes, thickly sliced

3 red peppers, deseeded and chopped

1 aubergine, chopped

2 red onions, chopped

5 shallots, peeled and quartered

250 g/9 oz button mushrooms

400 g/14 oz canned chopped tomatoes

1 tbsp tomato purée

50 g/1¾ oz butter

50 g/1¾ oz plain flour

600 ml/1 pint full-fat milk

100 g/3½ oz Cheddar cheese, grated

200 g/7 oz no-precook lasagne sheets

2 tbsp grated Parmesan cheese

salt and pepper

If using standard dried lasagne sheets, you will need to cook them according to the packet instructions before you start layering up the lasagne. Make sure that the lasagne sheets do not overlap.

Method

1 Preheat the oven to 190°C/375°F/Gas Mark 5. Put the oil in a large bowl, add the courgettes, peppers, aubergine, onions and shallots and toss well to coat.

2 Divide the vegetables between 2 baking trays and roast in the preheated oven for 30–40 minutes, until soft and flecked with brown. Add the button mushrooms after 20 minutes.

3 Remove the vegetables from the oven and tip into a large bowl. Add the tomatoes and tomato purée and mix well.

4 Melt the butter in a saucepan over a low heat. Stir in the flour and cook, stirring constantly, for 2–3 minutes. Gradually add the milk and cook, continuing to stir constantly, until the sauce is thick and smooth. Season to taste with salt and pepper and stir in the Cheddar cheese.

5 Layer the vegetable mixture and sauce in an ovenproof dish with the lasagne sheets, finishing with a layer of sauce. Sprinkle over the Parmesan cheese and bake in the preheated oven for 30–35 minutes.

6 Remove from the oven and serve hot.

risotto

Serves 4

Ingredients

2 litres/3½ pints stock or water

1 tbsp olive oil

3 tbsp butter

1 small onion, finely chopped

450 g/1 lb risotto rice

55 g/2 oz Parmesan cheese, finely grated

salt and pepper

Parmesan cheese shavings, to serve

Method

1 Bring the stock to the boil, then reduce the heat and keep simmering gently over a low heat while you are cooking the risotto. Heat the oil with 2 tablespoons of the butter in a deep saucepan over a medium heat until the butter has melted. Stir in the onion and cook gently until soft.

2 Add the rice and mix to coat in the oil and butter. Cook and stir for 2–3 minutes, or until the grains are translucent. Gradually add the stock, a ladleful at a time. Stir constantly and add more liquid as the rice absorbs it. Increase the heat to medium so that the liquid bubbles. Cook for 20 minutes, or until all the liquid is absorbed. The risotto should be of a creamy consistency with a bit of bite in the rice.

3 Remove the risotto from the heat and add the remaining butter. Mix well, then stir in the grated Parmesan cheese and season to taste with salt and pepper. Serve topped with Parmesan cheese shavings.

pasta with fresh pesto

Serves 4

Ingredients

about 40 fresh basil leaves

3 garlic cloves, crushed

25 g/1 oz pine kernels

50 g/1¾ oz Parmesan cheese, finely grated, plus extra to serve

2–3 tbsp extra virgin olive oil

350 g/12 oz dried pasta

salt and pepper

Method

1 Rinse the basil leaves and pat them dry with kitchen paper.

2 Place the basil leaves, garlic, pine kernels and grated Parmesan cheese in a tall beaker and process using a hand-held stick blender for 30 seconds, or until smooth. Alternatively, pound all of the ingredients by hand, using a pestle and mortar.

3 Gradually add the oil, stirring constantly, then season to taste with salt and pepper.

4 Bring a large saucepan of water to the boil. Add the pasta, return to the boil and cook for 8–10 minutes, until tender but still firm to the bite. Drain the pasta thoroughly, then transfer to a serving plate and serve with the pesto. Toss to mix well and serve hot, sprinkled with Parmesan.

This basic risotto recipe is infinitely versatile – just add your favourite ingredients to create your own special version.

stuffed red peppers with basil

Serves 4

Ingredients
140 g/5 oz long-grain white or brown rice

4 large red peppers

2 tbsp olive oil

1 garlic clove, chopped

4 shallots, chopped

1 celery stick, chopped

3 tbsp chopped toasted walnuts

2 tomatoes, peeled and chopped

1 tbsp lemon juice

50 g/1¾ oz raisins

4 tbsp freshly grated Cheddar cheese

2 tbsp chopped fresh basil

salt and pepper

You can use leftover cooked rice for this recipe. Try experimenting with different flavours, varying the nuts, dried fruit, cheese and herbs according to what you have to hand.

Method

1 Preheat the oven to 180°C/350°F/Gas Mark 4. Cook the rice in a saucepan of lightly salted boiling water for 20 minutes if using white rice, or 35 minutes if using brown. Drain, rinse under cold running water, then drain again.

2 Meanwhile, using a sharp knife, cut the tops off the peppers and reserve. Remove the seeds and white cores, then blanch the peppers and reserved tops in boiling water for 2 minutes. Remove from the heat and drain well. Heat half the oil in a large frying pan. Add the garlic and shallots and cook, stirring, for 3 minutes. Add the celery, walnuts, tomatoes, lemon juice and raisins and cook for a further 5 minutes. Remove from the heat and stir in the rice, cheese and basil and season to taste with salt and pepper.

3 Stuff the peppers with the rice mixture and arrange them in a baking dish. Place the tops on the peppers, drizzle over the remaining oil, loosely cover with foil and bake in the preheated oven for 45 minutes. Remove from the oven and serve.

STUDENT TASTE TEAM

Name: Anthony Trigo
Studying: History
At: Royal Holloway, London, UK
Comments about dish: This recipe was easy to make

Marks: 7/10

perfect roast potatoes

Serves 6

Ingredients

1.3 kg/3 lb large floury potatoes, peeled and cut into even-sized chunks

3 tbsp dripping, goose fat, duck fat or olive oil

salt

Method

1 Preheat the oven to 220°C/425°F/Gas Mark 7.

2 Cook the potatoes in a large saucepan of lightly salted boiling water over a medium heat, covered, for 5–7 minutes. They will still be firm. Remove from the heat. Meanwhile, add the fat to a roasting tin and place in the preheated oven.

3 Drain the potatoes well and return them to the saucepan. Cover and firmly shake the pan so that the surface of the potatoes is slightly roughened.

4 Remove the roasting tin from the oven and carefully tip the potatoes into the hot fat. Baste them to ensure that they are all coated with it.

5 Roast the potatoes at the top of the oven, turning once, for 45–50 minutes, or until they are browned all over.

6 Using a slotted spoon, carefully transfer the potatoes to a serving dish.

garlic mash

Serves 4

Ingredients

900 g/2 lb floury potatoes, peeled and cut into chunks

8 garlic cloves, crushed

150 ml/5 fl oz milk

85 g/3 oz butter

pinch of ground nutmeg

salt and pepper

1 tbsp chopped fresh flat-leaf parsley, to garnish

Method

1 Put the potatoes in a large saucepan. Add enough cold water to cover and a pinch of salt. Bring to the boil and cook for 10 minutes. Add the garlic and cook for a further 10 minutes, until the potatoes are tender.

2 Drain the potatoes and garlic thoroughly, reserving 3 tablespoons of the cooking liquid.

3 Return the reserved liquid to the pan, add the milk and bring to simmering point. Add the butter and return the potatoes and garlic to the pan. Mash thoroughly with a potato masher.

4 Season to taste with nutmeg, salt and pepper and beat the potato mixture with a wooden spoon until light and fluffy. Garnish with parsley and serve immediately.

vegetable rösti

Serves 4

Ingredients

1 carrot, peeled and grated

1 courgette, grated

1 sweet potato, peeled and grated

8 spring onions, finely chopped or shredded

1 egg white, beaten

2 tsp extra virgin olive oil

pepper

Method

1 Mix all the vegetables together, season to taste with pepper and stir in the egg white. Using clean hands, form into 8 small patties. Press them firmly together.

2 Heat the oil in a non-stick frying pan and cook the patties, in batches, over a gentle heat for 5–6 minutes, or until golden. Turn over halfway through the cooking time and press down with the back of a spatula.

cauliflower cheese

Serves 4

Ingredients

1 cauliflower, trimmed and cut into florets

40 g/1½ oz butter

40 g/1½ oz plain flour

450 ml/16 fl oz milk

115 g/4 oz Cheddar cheese, finely grated

pinch of ground nutmeg

1 tbsp grated Parmesan cheese

salt and pepper

Method

1 Cook the cauliflower in a saucepan of boiling water for 4–5 minutes. Drain and place in a baking dish.

2 Melt the butter in a saucepan over a medium heat and stir in the flour. Cook for 1 minute, stirring constantly, then remove from the heat and add the milk gradually until smooth. Return to a low heat, bring to the boil and simmer until the sauce is thick and creamy. Remove from the heat and stir in the Cheddar cheese and nutmeg. Season to taste with salt and pepper.

3 Preheat the grill. Pour the cheese sauce over the cauliflower, sprinkle over the Parmesan and place under the preheated grill to brown. Serve.

157

crumble

Serves 6

Ingredients
450 g/1 lb cooking apples
450 g/1 lb blackberries
115 g/4 oz caster sugar
4 tbsp water

Crumble topping
175 g/6 oz wholemeal flour
85 g/3 oz unsalted butter
85 g/3 oz soft light brown sugar
1 tsp mixed spice

Method
1 Preheat the oven to 190°C/375°F/Gas Mark 5. Prepare the apples by cutting them into quarters, then peeling and coring them. Thinly slice them into an ovenproof dish. Add the blackberries and then stir in the sugar. Pour over the water.

2 Make the crumble topping by placing the flour in a mixing bowl and rubbing in the butter until the mixture resembles breadcrumbs. Stir in the sugar and mixed spice. Spread the crumble evenly over the fruit and press down lightly.

3 Put the dish on a baking sheet and bake in the centre of the preheated oven for 25–30 minutes, until the crumble is golden brown.

This simple crumble recipe is easily adapted to include different fruits.

banana fritters

Serves 4

Ingredients
70 g/2½ oz plain flour
2 tbsp rice flour
1 tbsp caster sugar
1 egg, separated
150 ml/5 fl oz coconut milk
sunflower oil, for deep-frying
6 large bananas

To decorate/serve
1 tsp icing sugar
1 tsp ground cinnamon
lime wedges

Method
1 Sift the plain flour, rice flour and caster sugar into a bowl and make a well in the centre. Add the egg yolk and coconut milk. Beat the mixture until a smooth, thick batter forms.

2 Whisk the egg white in a clean, dry bowl until stiff enough to hold soft peaks. Fold it into the batter lightly and evenly.

3 Heat 6 cm/2½ inches of oil in a deep-fat fryer or large saucepan to 180–190°C/350–375°F, or until a cube of bread browns in 30 seconds. Cut the bananas in half crossways, then dip them quickly into the batter to coat them.

4 Drop the bananas carefully into the hot oil and deep-fry in batches for 2–3 minutes, until golden brown, turning once.

5 Drain on kitchen paper. Sprinkle with icing sugar and cinnamon and serve immediately, with lime wedges for squeezing over.

creamy rice pudding

Serves 4

Ingredients

butter, for greasing

85 g/3 oz sultanas, plus extra to decorate

5 tbsp caster sugar

90 g/3¼ oz pudding rice

1.2 litres/2 pints milk

1 tsp vanilla essence

finely grated rind of 1 large lemon

pinch of ground nutmeg

chopped pistachio nuts, to decorate

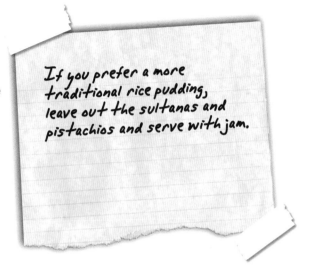

If you prefer a more traditional rice pudding, leave out the sultanas and pistachios and serve with jam.

Method

1 Preheat the oven to 160°C/325°F/Gas Mark 3. Grease an 850-ml/1½-pint ovenproof dish.

2 Put the sultanas, sugar and rice into a mixing bowl, then stir in the milk and vanilla essence. Transfer to the prepared dish, sprinkle over the lemon rind and nutmeg, then bake in the preheated oven for 2½ hours.

3 Remove from the oven and transfer to individual serving bowls. Decorate with sultanas and chopped pistachio nuts and serve.

chocolate mousse

Serves 4

Ingredients

300 g/10½ oz plain chocolate

1½ tbsp unsalted butter

1 tbsp brandy

4 eggs, separated

Method

1 Break the chocolate into small pieces and place in a heatproof bowl set over a pan of gently simmering water. (Make sure that the base of the bowl does not touch the water.) Add the butter and melt with the chocolate, stirring, until smooth. Remove from the heat, stir in the brandy and leave to cool slightly. Add the egg yolks and beat until smooth.

2 In a separate bowl, whisk the egg whites until stiff peaks have formed, then fold them into the chocolate mixture. Spoon the mixture into 4 small serving bowls and level the surfaces. Transfer to the refrigerator and chill for at least 4 hours, until set.

3 Take the mousse out of the refrigerator and serve.

quick tiramisù

Serves 4

Ingredients

225 g/8 oz mascarpone cheese or full-fat soft cheese

1 egg, separated

2 tbsp natural yogurt

2 tbsp caster sugar

2 tbsp dark rum

2 tbsp cold strong black coffee

8 sponge fingers

2 tbsp grated plain chocolate

Method

1 Put the mascarpone cheese, egg yolk and yogurt in a large bowl and beat together until smooth.

2 Whisk the egg white in a separate bowl until stiff peaks have formed, then whisk in the sugar and gently fold into the cheese mixture. Divide half the mixture between 4 sundae glasses.

3 Mix the rum and coffee together in a shallow dish. Dip the sponge fingers into the rum mixture, break them in half, or into smaller pieces if necessary, and divide between the glasses.

4 Stir any remaining coffee mixture into the remaining cheese mixture and divide between the glasses.

5 Sprinkle with the grated chocolate. Serve immediately or cover and chill in the refrigerator until required.

Eating raw eggs should be avoided by infants, the elderly, pregnant women, convalescents and anyone suffering from an illness.

useful
stuff

If you are new to cooking, you might discover that there are techniques and equipment mentioned in recipes that you are unfamiliar with. You may find yourself asking 'What's the difference between *boiling* and *simmering*?' or 'What on earth is a *mortar and pestle*?'. Well, this section has the answers to those questions and many more. It will increase your understanding of *cooking jargon* and help you onto the path to becoming an experienced and knowledgeable cook.

PREPARATION TECHNIQUES

This section, arranged in handy alphabetical order, is a valuable source of reference for all the preparation techniques you are likely to find in everyday cooking.

Baste

When you spoon juices or fat over a food during cooking, this is known as 'basting'. It helps to keep the food moist and seal in the flavour.

Beat

This technique involves using a fork, spoon or electric mixer in a vigorous stirring motion to remove any lumps from sauces and incorporate air.

Blend

Blending involves combining two or more ingredients together by stirring with a spoon or puréeing with an electric blender.

Chop

This means to cut food into small pieces using a sharp knife. You can chop food roughly or finely depending on the dish you are cooking. Roughly chopped means that the food will be left in larger pieces than when finely chopped.

Cream

Creaming is similar to beating in that you use a fork, spoon or electric mixer to beat ingredients together until they are smooth. This technique is usually associated with ingredients that are rich and creamy, such as butter.

Crush

This technique is useful for bringing out the flavour of garlic and herbs, and can be done by pressing the flat side of a knife blade down onto the garlic or herbs.

Cut

This method means to use a sharp knife to make an incision or separate a food into smaller pieces.

Dice

This means to cut food into regular-shaped cubes using a sharp knife.

Fold

This technique involves mixing a light mixture into a heavier one using a spoon or spatula in a figure-of-eight movement. This is done to keep the air in the mixture.

Grate

To shred food into small pieces using a grater.

Grease/oil

This is to rub a little butter or oil over the surface of a pan or tin to prevent food from sticking to it during cooking.

Grind

To crush food, such as nuts or spices, to a powder or into very small pieces. You can use a pestle and mortar for a coarser result, or a coffee grinder or food processor.

Julienne

This technique involves cutting food, such as carrots and celery, into fine batons or strips.

Knead

This technique uses the heel of the hand to pull and stretch bread in order to develop the gluten in the flour so that the bread will keep its shape when it has risen.

Knock back

This means to knock the air out of bread dough after it has risen.

Marinate

This term means to soak food in a marinade in order to tenderize it and give it more flavour. You can marinate meat, poultry, fish and vegetables.

Mash

Mashing means to reduce food, often cooked potatoes or other root vegetables, to a pulp using a potato masher or fork.

Peel

Peeling involves removing the outer skin or rind from foods, such as oranges, avocados or potatoes. Depending on the food, you can use your hands, a sharp knife or a vegetable peeler.

Purée

This describes reducing food to a smooth pulp. You can do this by pushing food through a sieve or using a blender.

Rub in

This technique is mainly used in making pastry. Using the fingertips, rub the fat into the flour, lifting it high over the basin in order to trap air into the mixture.

Score

This term means to make light incisions on the surface of a food, especially meat, poultry or fish, in order to facilitate cooking, allow any fat to drain and create a decorative effect.

Shred

This technique involves using a small, sharp knife or grater to cut food into very thin lengths.

Sift

This technique involves shaking dry ingredients, such as flour, through a sieve to remove lumps and introduce air into the mixture.

Snip

This means to use kitchen scissors to cut leafy green vegetables or herbs into very small pieces.

Whisk

Whisking involves beating a light mixture, such as cream or eggs, vigorously with a whisk to incorporate more air. You can use a balloon whisk, an electric hand mixer or a food processor with a whisk attachment.

Zest

This means to remove the outer layer of citrus fruit. A zester takes off the zest without picking up the bitter white pith underneath.

COOKING METHODS

From traditional cooking techniques, such as boiling and roasting, to more contemporary ones, like steaming and stir-frying, there are many different ways to cook food. This section summarizes some of the most popular ones.

Bake

This technique involves cooking food in an oven using dry heat.

Blanch

To plunge a food into boiling water for a few minutes, then remove and place in iced water. This technique is often used to preserve the colour and texture of vegetables, and to loosen the skins of nuts, tomatoes and other fruits.

Boil

This means to cook food in a liquid (usually water, stock or milk) in a saucepan at boiling point (100°C/212°F). Not all foods are boiled continuously – sometimes they are 'brought to the boil', then the temperature is reduced and the food is left to simmer. This method is also used to 'reduce' a liquid or sauce (i.e. to evaporate off any excess moisture and make the sauce thicker).

Braise

This is a long, slow way to cook food and is especially useful for tough cuts of meat. To braise foods, first brown them in oil, then cook them very slowly in a small amount of flavoured liquid in a saucepan or dish with a tight-fitting lid. You can cook them on the hob or in the oven.

Deep-fry

This involves immersing food completely in very hot oil and cooking it at a very high temperature. It can be dangerous as it is possible to spill the hot oil or the pan can catch fire, so great care must be taken and the pan should never be left unattended. A thermostatically-controlled deep-fat fryer is a safer and easier option, but this still needs care and attention during use.

Dry-fry

This means to cook food, such as nuts or spices, without using fat or oil to colour it lightly.

Grill

Grilling food involves cooking it directly under the heat source. Most cookers come with an integral grill, as well as a grill pan with a wire mesh to allow excess fat to drain away.

Poach

Poaching means to cook food in a liquid at just below boiling point. You can poach poultry, fish, eggs and fruit.

Roast

Roasting is similar to baking, in that a food is cooked in the oven using dry heat, and is often used for meat, poultry and vegetables. It is usually necessary to add a little fat when roasting foods to keep them moist.

Sauté

This is similar to shallow-frying, but with less oil. It also involves moving the food around to prevent it from browning too quickly.

Shallow-fry

This method uses less oil than deep-frying and is suitable for foods that will not burn easily – for example, foods that are coated in flour, breadcrumbs or batter. The food is not moved around the pan during cooking, but may be turned over halfway through.

Simmer

To simmer means to cook food in liquid that is just below boiling point – there will be very gentle bubbles on the surface of the liquid.

Steam

This means to cook a food with steam, either using a metal or bamboo steamer placed inside a pan containing a small amount of water or an electric steamer. It is a very healthy cooking method because the food doesn't come into contact with the liquid and therefore more of the nutrients are preserved.

Stir-fry

This originates in Asia and is a quick and healthy method of cooking. Foods, such as meat, poultry and vegetables, are cut into small, similar-sized pieces and cooked quickly in a little hot oil, whilst being tossed constantly. You can use a wok or a large frying pan for stir-frying, but a wok is better because its shape means that the food is cooked more rapidly as it comes into contact with the hot sides of the wok.

TABLE OF EQUIVALENTS

Oven Temperatures

°C	°F	Gas
110	225	
120	250	¼
140	275	½
150	300	1
160	325	2
180	350	3
190	375	4
200	400	5
220	425	6
230	450	7
240	475	8
		9

Liquid Measures

1 teaspoon (tsp)	4.6207 millilitres (ml)
1 tablespoon (tbsp)	18.4829 millilitres
½ pint	284 millilitres
1 pint	568 millilitres

Dry Measures

1 ounce (oz)	28 grams (g)
1 pound (lb)	454 grams
2.2046 pounds	1 kilogram (kg)

Length

1 millimetre (mm)	0.0394 inch (in)
1 centimetre (cm)	0.3937 inch
2.54 cm	1 inch

EQUIPMENT

You may find that your student kitchen is already kitted out with a range of basic utensils or, on the other hand, you might not be that lucky. Either way, it's worth having a few carefully chosen kitchen tools of your own that you can take with you when you move on to new accommodation. When you are starting out, you can make do with a few multi-purpose utensils, then add to them as your confidence and repertoire grow.

Baking dish

An ovenproof dish, often ceramic, that is used for cooking food in the oven.

Baking sheets and trays

These are flat metal sheets, sometimes with a rim around the edges. They are essential for baking a variety of foods.

Bottle opener/corkscrew

Essential for opening bottles of wine or beer, you can buy these individually or combined into one utensil.

Cake tins

A cake tin is an essential item if you want to bake a cake. Always use the size specified in the recipe.

Can opener

Although many tins and cans now come with handy ring pulls, this is a useful tool to have in your kitchen drawer.

Casserole dish

This is handy for cooking casseroles, pot-roasts and stews in the oven. A flameproof casserole may also be used over direct heat on the hob to brown food before being transferred to the oven.

Chopping boards

Essential for protecting the work surface when you are cutting foods, these are available in a range of different materials. Ideally, you should keep a separate board for raw meat and poultry.

Colander

A colander is a perforated bowl that is used for draining liquid from foods, such as pasta.

Deep-fat fryer

This machine is used for deep-frying foods, such as chips. It is safer than deep-frying using a saucepan as it regulates the temperature of the oil, but should still be used with great care and never left unattended.

Frying pan

This is like a saucepan, only shallower. A small frying pan is useful for cooking omelettes, whilst a large one can be used for more substantial foods.

Garlic press

This utensil is used for crushing garlic cloves cleanly and efficiently. If you don't have one, you can crush garlic by pressing down on the garlic clove with the side of a heavy knife.

Grater

This is used for shredding foods, such as cheese, vegetables and chocolate. A hollow box-shaped grater is a good multi-purpose tool as it has different-sized cutting holes on each side, allowing you to grate finely or coarsely depending on the recipe.

Griddle pan

Although not essential, a ridged griddle pan gives food a lovely stripy effect and is ideal for cooking steaks.

Hand-held stick blender

This electrical item is a portable version of a blender and allows you to purée foods, such as soups, in the saucepan, saving on washing up. It is also useful for making smoothies and dips.

Kitchen scissors

Scissors have all sorts of uses in the kitchen – for example, they are handy for chopping meat into small pieces and for snipping herbs. Choose stainless-steel all-purpose scissors and keep them especially for use in the kitchen.

Knives

There is a huge range of different knives available. For everyday cooking, a small paring knife, a long cook's knife and a long, serrated bread knife should be adequate.

Lemon squeezer

This is used for extracting the juice from citrus fruits, such as lemons and limes. The most common type has a cone onto which you press the halved fruit and a bowl to catch the juice. Some have a built-in strainer to catch the pips.

Measuring jug

This is a clear jug, usually made from toughened plastic or glass, with markers up the side. It is used for measuring liquids. When checking a measurement, place the jug on a flat surface at eye level.

Measuring spoons

These spoons are ideal for measuring both liquid and dry ingredients accurately. For everyday cooking, you can use ordinary kitchen spoons but be aware that they can vary in size quite substantially.

Mixing bowls

Mixing bowls are available in a variety of materials. It is useful to have at least one large and one small.

Pastry brush

Pastry brushes are handy for brushing glazes onto foods. They can also be used for greasing and oiling bakeware to prevent food from sticking during cooking.

Pestle and mortar

These two utensils come as a pair – the bowl is called the mortar and stick is the pestle. They are used for grinding foods, such as nuts and spices.

Potato masher

This utensil is used for crushing potatoes and other root vegetables until they are smooth.

Roasting tins

These metal tins are deeper than baking trays, and are ideal for roasting meat and poultry.

Saucepans

Saucepans are used for cooking foods over direct heat on the hob. It is good to have them in a variety of sizes so you have a suitable one for each different job. Choose saucepans with well-fitting lids.

Scales

Kitchen scales come in manual and electronic versions. They are an essential piece of kit if you plan to do any baking because the ingredients will need to be measured accurately.

Sieve

Like colanders, sieves are used for draining foods, although their holes are much finer than those on a colander. Sieves are useful for sifting flour to remove lumps.

Skewers

These are long metal or wooden sticks that are used to skewer meats and other ingredients to make kebabs. Wooden skewers should be soaked before use to stop them burning.

Slotted spoon

This is a large spoon with holes or slots in it. It is ideal for lifting foods out of liquids so that the liquid drains away.

Timer

A kitchen timer is handy for monitoring cooking times and will sound an alarm when the time is up. Many ovens have built-in timers.

Tongs

A set of tongs is perfect for gripping and turning hot foods.

Vegetable peeler

You can peel vegetables or fruit with a knife, but vegetable peelers make the job easier and safer. There are various different styles of vegetable peeler, from swivel-bladed to Y-shaped.

Whisk

Hand whisks are useful for whisking ingredients, such as cream, to incorporate air into them. If you don't have one, you can use a fork or a spoon but it will take a lot longer.

Wire cooling racks

These metal racks are used to allow air to circulate around baked goods, such as biscuits and cakes, as they cool so that they don't become soggy.

Wok

A large bowl-shaped pan used in Asian cuisine, the wok's curved sides make it perfect for stir-frying. If you don't have one, a deep frying pan or large saucepan can be used instead.

Wooden spoon

Wooden spoons are used for mixing ingredients together. They are handy for stirring hot foods as they don't conduct heat in the way that metal spoons do. Also, they won't scratch delicate surfaces on pans.

Index